FRESH GROUND
& RE-CAFFINATED

D0807916

STEVEN WARD

THE
COFFEEIST
MANIFESTO

Learn How to Make Coffee YOURSELF: The Coffeeist Manifesto

2nd Edition by Steven Ward

Steven@CoffeeistManifesto.com

Published by Manifesto Digital Media LLC, 412 N Main St Suite 100, Buffalo, WY, 82834. ManifestoDigitalMedia.com, Info@ManifestoDigitalMedia.com

Additional resources for readers can be found via CoffeeistManifesto.com/readers

Originally published as The Coffeeist Manifesto: No More Bad Coffee! In 2012

ISBN-13: 978-0692588338
ISBN-10: 0692588337

"...The favorite drink of the civilised world."
-Thomas Jefferson

Contents

INTRODUCTION

I made a deliberate decision in the writing of this book to defy convention. If you look at other books in the coffee genre, they are dripping with romance and have book covers featuring calming, but neutral, browns and beiges and lots and lots of pictures of coffee in fancy cups.

Who doesn't enjoy the atmosphere of a cool neighborhood coffee shop? Even my wife, whose stomach is too sensitive for coffee, greatly enjoys the smell as I prepare it in the morning. And yes, some of the latte artists out there can produce jaw-dropping images out of milk foam. I completely understand why most authors choose to highlight the aesthetic value of coffee and aim to mystify and romanticize it.

But this mystification is a double-edged sword. The over-emphasis of these pleasurable aspects of coffee puts it on a pedestal that does all of us a disservice. It dissuades people from learning more and takes away from the aesthetic pleasure involved with all steps in the preparation of coffee. More than this, it encourages ignorance of where that coffee comes from.

This book focuses on bringing coffee back to the people. Coffee goes through a long, winding path to end up in our cups and that path is becoming ever more obscured as we thoughtlessly sling back mug-fulls of swill that has had its natural qualities drowned by artificial sweetener, milk, and flavored syrups. This all happens, of course, after the beans have been burnt to a crisp and put in storage long enough to go stale and bitter before you ever lay eyes on it in the grocery store.

The beans, which easily could have been grown on a farm owned by the same family for centuries, were likely to be hand picked by farm hands living in poverty, but at least by doing so they can provide a meager living for their family.

That cup of coffee in your hand connects the ancient world with the modern; the barista and the consumer; the small batch micro-roasting hobbyist and their friends and relatives that enjoy getting fresh roasted coffee as gifts. Coffee is a drink of the people and should always be honored as such.

This book seeks to demystify coffee and bring it down off its pedestal, while recognizing that coffee does indeed hold a special place in the history of modern civilization. It will separate facts from fiction and try to give a solid foundation in the art of coffee appreciation.

While I expect that the topics in this book will appeal to many people, it is an intensely personal project for me. I never set out to become any sort of authority on coffee. Rather, I was simply trying to improve my quality of life. This book is framed by my own extensive research and experience and you will not find another book on the topic that puts this information together in such a concise, no-BS way.

I love coffee because for a few minutes every day I put all of my focus and energy into the creation of something great. I enjoy it for a few minutes, but then it's gone. Until tomorrow when I start the whole process all over again. On any given day, that morning cup might be your last, so you'd better give it your all. Making a great cup of coffee is a perfect work of Zen art.

The topic of this book may be making coffee, but the subtext message I want to put out into the universe is one of always taking the time to appreciate the small things and never take anyone for granted, whether it's your spouse, your friends, your parents, the barista that makes your espresso, or the farmer that grows the coffee beans. Treat every conversation and every relationship as if it, just like that perfect cup of coffee, were a precious work of temporary Zen art. Because it is.

For H, J, and G

CHAPTER ONE

The Big Picture

Coffeeists of the World, Unite!

The coffee bourgeois has deceived us. They have convinced us that making amazing coffee for ourselves is beyond our capability. They have inserted themselves into our lives without being invited and demanded payment for the privilege of having them there. And for what? Not only are we used to a final product that is stale, bitter, and over-priced, but we do not even realize that we have been deceived.

Indeed, the world of coffee is as nuanced and complex as that of wine. While the multi-billion dollar coffee corporations have convinced us that the equivalent of stale box wine is the epitome of the coffee experience, the reality is that, with a modicum of effort, we could be enjoying complex aromas and nuances on par with that of a fine French Bordeaux every day, all the while saving money in the long run.

They are able to do this because, for most of us, coffee is an afterthought. We mindlessly consume it on a first date, or while studying for an exam, or over breakfast at our favorite greasy spoon. We really don't even think about where it came from, the backbreaking labor of the farmers, or the trip around the world it took to get it to us. I call this being a coffee zombie.

For years, I, too, was a coffee zombie. I loved coffee, but thought of it first and foremost as a drug. I was stubbornly proud that I drank it black, out of a sort of ignorant machismo. I "enjoyed" coffee by drinking it dark and bitter to show how much of a man I was because it was actually terrible. I didn't realize it at the time, but I was drinking stale beans that were burnt to a crisp.

I was woefully ignorant about the world of coffee, but that didn't stop me from being a complete snob. I bought into the notion that "good" coffee is dark and bitter. I thought I knew all there was to know about coffee, but actually I knew next to nothing. Frankly, there was a lot of encouragement in modern culture to remain blissfully, proudly, ignorant. I could have easily been mistaken for a real zombie the way I would stumble haphazardly around in a daze until I got my morning fix. Thankfully, unlike being a real zombie, it is possible to recover.

As I explored the world of coffee, starting with books and blogs, what stuck out in my mind was how much elitism and snobbery there was out there. So much of the literature seemed to be about showing off how knowledgable the author was. As I learned more and more, eventually attending trade shows and reading academic articles related to coffee, I started to see the cracks in the knowledge of the snobs. Like any blowhard, when there was a gap in their knowledge they would fill it in with extrapolation and educated guesses, but try and pass it off to others as fact.

Now, when I say "elitist" I'm not talking about coffee experts with decades of experience in the industry here. I'm talking about your friend that studied abroad in Italy for a semester and now likes to show off her encyclopedic knowledge of espresso by bringing it up every chance she gets. But my point is not to demonize these people. Rather, I want to reach out to them. If nothing else, I hope *The Coffeeist Manifesto* is received as a call for humility when it comes to coffee. Let's all just chill out and not take ourselves too seriously.

As my knowledge and experience progressed, I found myself offended by the presence of coffee academies and the like. They charged big money to teach people how to pour water through a filter and into a cup. Who needs a fancy framed certificate for that nonsense?

This crystalized in my mind just how serious the elitism is in the world of coffee. Thinking back on my own experiences, I now see that the problem is the information gaps. As easy as it is to make and enjoy awesome coffee, the current literature is mostly either so narrow in scope that only professional baristas and coffee shop owners would give a damn about it or so filled with sappy fluff that you'd fall asleep trying to read it. The gap in the literature is huge. Coffee lovers wanting to learn a little more about coffee without getting overwhelmed with discussions of the best amount of air pressure for making perfectly extracted espresso had to fend for themselves doing research on the Internet.

I want to try and connect all the dots for you and give you a road map for the enjoyment of coffee. I'm sick and tired of stuck-up baristas, elitist web forums, and greedy "coffee academy" owners telling us we need to take their expensive classes in order to learn more. I'm sorry, but that's crap. For those of us that likely won't ever own a coffee shop, the idea that we need to pay hundreds of dollars of our hard-earned money for someone to show us the proper technique for pouring a liquid into a cup is absurd.

Although it might not be intentional, there is a big lie that permeates our culture in regards to making great coffee: Making amazing coffee is hard and requires special training / a certain expensive machine / magical powers. It's just not true.

With time, I had a hard time describing my

interest in coffee to people. Telling people "I like coffee," is an understatement. While some friends of mine have referred to me casually as an "expert" I cringe at the word because I've never had any type of professional investment in the coffee world. It was after I started writing this book that the term "Coffeeist" came to me as a fusion of coffee and enthusiast.

Join me, fellow coffeeists, in the next great cultural revolution. We will take back the power, protect our wallets, and enrich our lives by educating ourselves in a way that does not seek to elevate ourselves to elitism, but to help each other appreciate the ritual, the sights, and the sounds of coffee and, by extension, the other little things in life.

Comrades, in today's world, that is a revolutionary act.

A Brief History of Coffee

Given coffee's revolutionary history, it is a shame how mainstream, pedestrian and *bad* most coffee is today. When I say that coffee has a revolutionary history, I mean, literally, revolutionary.

Whether it is myth or fact, the discovery of the coffee bean is largely attributed to a young goat herder in Ethiopia named Kaldi (and yes, there are hundreds of coffee shops that use the name "Kaldi"). Supposedly young Kaldi's goats had been eating coffee cherries and, high on the world's first caffeine buzz, were bouncing off the walls. Kaldi finally figured out that it was this mysterious cherry that had caused them to act loopy, so he tried it himself.

Though Kaldi enjoyed the effects of eating the cherry (and, critically important, the seed inside the cherry), there's a reason we don't eat coffee cherries or green (unroasted) beans: They don't particularly taste good. Or so I've heard.

Although coffee snobs the world over, including myself, insist that their obsession over coffee is not about the caffeine hit, it seems clear that the first efforts at coffee making were all about finding the most effective caffeine delivery system. It is generally understood to have been religious figures that figured this part out and oversaw coffee's expansion into the Middle East where the first coffee shops started springing up sometime in the middle of the second millennium.[1]

Thus began coffee's history of being associated with rebels and troublemakers. Although it was generally accepted by Islam, the monarchs of the day didn't trust people gathering in coffee shops, ingesting a mild stimulant, and talking for hours on end. One even took it upon himself to roam the streets in disguise, beheading anyone he saw with a cup of coffee.

Coffee continued to be popular despite attempts to ban and eradicate it. Eventually, it caught on in Europe, where beer was staple beverage even over water. It is estimated that medieval Europeans consumed around two six packs worth of beer every day, often gathering in pubs and such to partake of the nectar socially.[2]

So it's not a big stretch of the imagination to see how introducing the stimulant of caffeine to a population accustomed only to the depressant alcohol might cause some ripples. At least one author claims that, in fact, the Renaissance itself, for which we owe much of modern science, art, culture, and democracy, was born out of the ideas that came up in conversations held over cups of coffee in the newly introduced coffee shops.

It may surprise you to learn that the people of North America, at one point in time, drank far more tea than they did coffee. This preceded the existence of Canada and the United States, although the transition to coffee did mirror a critical moment in the history of the continent: the Boston Tea Party. That milestone event put the thirteen colonies and England on a path to the Revolutionary War and it also facilitated the rejection of tea as the new country's national drink. From then on, plans were hatched and big ideas were discussed over steaming hot cups of coffee.

The renaissance of coffee in North America and other places in the world, in terms of taste, is a recent phenomenon thanks to (are you sitting down?) Starbucks. Say what you will about the massive corporate behemoth, but the company has popularized what was previously a very niche industry and made words like cappuccino and cafe latte part of our vocabularies.

Purists may argue that in addition to popularizing these drinks, they have also cheapened and bastardized them, but Starbucks deserves a lot of credit. For every indie cafe that went out of business when a Starbucks opened across the street, there is probably another cafe a couple blocks away that never could have existed had Starbucks not popularized coffee and brought us out of the dark ages of pre-ground, canned, and, even worse, instant, coffee.

When most people talk about buying a cup of coffee, there's a strong possibility they're picturing a Starbucks in their head. As of June 29th, 2012, there are almost 20,000 locations spread over 59 countries.[3] They are the biggest name in the game and as such, they have a big sign painted on their back. They are an easy target.

While some of the criticism Starbucks gets may be warranted, frankly, some is not. One thing I can say is that fans of coffee of all stripes, from the most hardcore of the hoity toities to the instant coffee-drinking average Joes, owe a debt of gratitude to the education Starbucks has given the world about coffee. Before Starbucks, Folgers and Maxwell House were the biggest names around. With Starbucks now an ubiquitous presence on seemingly every street corner on earth, it has forced everyone to step up their game. A few years ago, Consumer Reports announced that McDonald's, yes, McDonald's, coffee has surpassed Starbucks.[4] I can't disagree more strongly with this assessment, but it's certainly true the McDonald's has taken great strides to improve the quality of the coffee they serve.

In fact, in the tiny country of South Korea, McDonald's has recently announced an ambitious plan for the aggressive expansion of its McCafe coffee shops around the country.⁵ In a pre-Starbucks world, would a company like McDonald's even bother trying to improve its coffee? It's hard to say. While McCafe's might not stand up to the high standards of specialty coffee connoisseurs, consider this: When I first visited Seoul in the year 2000, it was nearly impossible to find fresh roasted coffee. But six years later, when I came back during grad school after Starbucks' aggressive expansion throughout the country, I noticed more neighborhood cafes starting to pop up. By 2008 it wasn't hard at all to find small independent coffee shops with their own roasters.

Starbucks has even upped the ante in the instant coffee game with the introduction of Via instant coffee, which uses a mixture of traditionally freeze-dried instant coffee and "micro-ground" coffee grounds.

Although I believe in giving credit where credit is due, I'm certainly not a Starbucks apologist. Aside from the positive effects Starbucks has had on the coffee world, there are some well-deserved criticisms aimed at the corporation:

1) Anti-competitive market strategies may be the number one criticism of the company. "Buying out competitors' leases, intentionally operating at a loss, and clustering several locations in a small

geographical area,'"[6] are three such practices the chain is criticized for.

2) Starbucks also takes heat over its labor policies. Starbucks has paid large settlements in labor disputes with pro-union employees, though the have not admitted any wrongdoing in these cases.[7] Additionally, a supposed corporate policy stipulates that tips are shared with managers, which is illegal in some places and has resulted in some big payouts.[8] I was surprised to find out that a lot of people are unhappy with Starbucks' labor practices, as my impression had been that Starbucks goes out of their way to offer education programs and insurance benefits even to part-time employees, but that impression was developed from CEO Howard Shultz's book,[9] so I guess it should be taken with a grain of salt.

In my humble opinion, these two criticisms have strong merits. Some other hot button issues are Starbucks' stated support for gay marriage and, in places with conceal and carry gun laws, not requiring customers to disarm themselves before coming inside. Depending on where you fall on these issues they could be either positives or negatives. I still think Starbucks has done more good than bad though. I'm sure there are a whole lot of specialty coffee shops that would never have existed if Starbucks hadn't laid the groundwork by educating the public in the basic language of espressos and lattes.

Generally speaking, I try to avoid Starbucks, but it's not because of any of the above criticisms. Rather, in pursuit of my own enjoyment of coffee, I look for more varied experiences. I'm willing to take a chance on a place a couple blocks away that I've never tried before rather than the Starbucks right in front of me where I can expect a predictable, if not spectacular, experience. In other words, the idea of patronizing any large megolithic corporate coffee chain at all goes against the very thing I love about coffee: experimentation.

Still, whenever I'm visiting family in Missouri, I'm very grateful for the several Starbucks' around town.[10] While the Main Street Cafe in Independence is decent and I always try to visit The Roasterie (it has been listed on various lists of the best coffee shops in the country) in Kansas City, I usually end up patronizing the Starbucks down the street more often than I'd care to admit.

The Rise of Specialty Coffee

Specialty Coffee, otherwise known as "third wave" coffee, has flourished since the rise of Starbucks, thanks in no small measure to the education that Starbucks has given the world.

For many people, a Starbucks opening in their town was their first introduction to something better than the canned, pre-ground, coffee they grew up on. After becoming accustomed to Starbucks and the strange foreign language of lattes and cappuccinos, many of those same people were primed and ready to make a second leap in their coffee enjoyment, priming them for a new type of coffee shop.

You can think of specialty coffee in the same vein as a craft brewery or artisan bakery. They are typically independent, locally-owned shops deeply committed to serving high quality coffee.

When one of these places, typically associated with being 'hipster' opens near you, it's something to be excited about. Later in the book, I'll offer tips on how to identify a true specialty coffee shop from one that's just trying to capitalize on coffee's recent popularity.

Politics

It is worth discussing some political issues in the world of coffee at a little greater length, because the fact remains that while we enjoy our coffee in our comfortable homes and trendy coffee shops, many of the people that made that cup of perfection possible are living in near destitute conditions. If that's not bad enough, coffee farming seems to have serious consequences for the environment, especially in terms of deforestation, driving out endangered species (especially birds) and the use of harsh chemicals and pesticides that are bad for the land and even worse for the farmers and their families.

While this section gets a little dense and slightly academic, I wanted to present the basics of the issues. I'm not going to push everyone to run out and start drinking organic coffee exclusively, but I do think people should at least understand what the basic issues are, including arguments both for and against, so that they can make their own decisions.

"Free trade" in coffee was put to an end in 1971, with the establishment of the International Coffee Agreement, the treaty that established the International Coffee Organization. The coffee importing and exporting countries of the world saw a need to collaborate in controlling the coffee trade in response to the attempts Brazil made in the early twentieth century to fight off competitors after establishing itself as the world's leading coffee producer.[11] The official ICO story, however, is that protection was needed against a reoccurring cycle in the coffee prices due to producers over-planting to try and make up for losses in the previous year.[12]

The fundamental issue the ICO tries to address is the wild swings in coffee prices by enforcing quotas and it does so by bringing together both importing and exporting countries to sit down and work out an across the board buying price and quota. In principle, this keeps Brazil from producing too many coffee beans, which would then presumably tank the price as there would be far more supply than demand. Traditionally (the most recent ICA does not include the quota system)[13], the ICO has set the amount of coffee it will accept from a given export country and the price that the importing country will pay for it. At first glance, it sounds like a good thing that the market is kept somewhat stable to ensure a certain price. However, research out of the Department of Agriculture and Resource Economics at the University of California-Davis in 1999 states:

"Econometric analysis supports the hypothesis that use of quotas resulted in lower producer prices in most coffee producing countries. The income lost by producers was largely captured by governments and/or exporters to whom the governments assigned quota rights. Since coffee is produced by small farmers in most exporting countries, income distribution within those countries probably worsened.[14]"

Other research backed this finding up by showing that while the coffee exporting countries are all on equal footing in terms of the quotas for production, within the individual countries there was variation in policies and how much of a split of the set price actually made it to the producers.[15] Hopefully we've seen the last of the quota system. The larger point I'm trying to make is that the ICO does, in fact, exert influence over the coffee trade to control prices. I include this little bit of ammo just in case someone gives you the economic argument against Fair Trade coffee.

In theory, coffee producers are not *required* to sell through ICO buyers and are still able to sell on the open market. In practice, however, that's easier said than done for a small family farm with limited resources. In Kenya, the government is pretty much the only buyer and producers may not receive their payments for the coffee until up to a year later, though they are still held responsible for late payments on their government sponsored loans that were used to pay for processing equipment, irrigation, etc.[16] In other countries, while producers are not forced to sell to ICO buyers, there are likely very few options.

In all this mess, someone, somewhere, first had the idea of trying to improve bottom lines of the producers and protect the environment of the plantations through the development of certifications.

You may have heard of these three types of coffee certifications, even if you didn't understand them:

- Organic
- Shade—Grown
- Fair Trade

These three labels have nothing to do with the taste of the coffee, nor do they relate to the species of the coffee tree. The first two simply relate to the method of growing the coffee (confronting environmental impacts), while the third is strictly related to the coffee trade itself (economic). Usually the presence of any of the above has a direct correlation with the price of the coffee.

Chances are you are already somewhat familiar with the term "organic" and its connotations. While regulatory agencies in various countries have different standards, the idea is that no chemicals are used in the growing of the bean. That's not just pesticides, but also fertilizers.

But one does not just declare themselves organic and start printing green stickers. There's a strict certification process. The United States Department of Agriculture requires:

"In order for coffee to be certified and sold as organic in the United States, it must be produced in accordance with U.S. standards for organic production and certified by an agency accredited by the U.S. Department of Agriculture. U.S. requirements for organic coffee production include farming without synthetic pesticides or other prohibited substances for three years and a sustainable crop rotation plan to prevent erosion, the depletion of soil nutrients, and control for pests.[17]"

As you can imagine, this is a costly and lengthy process for farmers to go through. In some scholars' assessments, the certification process leads to lower quality coffee because it places further burden on already hardworking farmers.[18] All in all, the jury is still out on organic coffee, though there are people working very hard to make it work.

For those concerned about the environment, this has important connotations. It does not, however, factor in the quality of the coffee. Some may claim that they can detect a taste difference between organic and regular beans. They might be right. What I mean is that there is no test for quality or taste in the certification process. At least in the case of the USDA, as of this writing.

I'm sure there are some amazing organic coffee beans out there and I'm just as sure that there are less than amazing organic beans. The point is, if you're only buying organic in the *untested* belief that you are getting better coffee, it is pretty likely you are mistaken.

Certified shade—grown coffee, sometimes sold as "Bird Friendly" coffee refers to growing coffee using a method of farming that many believe prevents deforestation. By growing the coffee under a canopy of trees, you aren't cutting down forests and destroying the natural habitat of tropical birds (which may or may not be endangered as the case may be) in the name of coffee farming.

Shade—grown coffee is not organic coffee. In fact, shade—grown coffee generally requires intensive pesticides and chemicals to nurture it. Until they can figure out a way to cut out the chemicals, organic and shade-grown coffee methods are competing philosophies at environmental sustainability. Unlike organic coffee, there is still no organized effort to certify or otherwise vouch for shade—grown coffee. Some literature even suggests that shade—grown coffee doesn't promote biodiversity as it claims to, due to generally using the same types of trees as 'shade' on the plantations.[19]

While the previous two certification programs

address environmental impacts, the Free Trade coffee certification specifically seeks to protect labor and trade standards.[20] Although FT coffee is not necessarily organic or shade—grown, there is a lot of overlap and 59 percent of all FT coffee sold in 2008 was also organic.[21] The FT certification system does include some environmental sustainability restrictions against "the use of genetically modified organisms (GMOs) and the most hazardous pesticides."[22]

Additionally, while it might seem as though, given the stringent requirements a producer must fulfill to be certified, these systems are cases of the First World feeling guilty about picking up a latte in the drive thru lane with their SUV while the farmers that made the coffee can't even send their kids away to school. At least in the case of Mexico, the genesis of organic certification was a 15-year grassroots effort brought about through "populist agrarian organizing and accompanying organizational innovations."[23] Research published in the Journal of Agriculture and Environmental Ethics took this a step further by comparing the priorities of the coffee trade historically against the new "alternative trade organizations":

"An examination of the philosophies of the fair trade and organic coffee movements reveal that the philosophical underpinnings of both certified organic and fair-trade coffee run counter to the historical concerns of coffee production and trade."[24]

All this aside, does organic/shade--grown/free trade coffee TASTE better? Maybe. To be perfectly honest, I haven't personally noticed a huge difference in taste. Again, it's up to your own tastes. However there is a strong argument that having a variety of species of tall trees providing the shade contributes to healthy soil and higher quality coffee beans, but I don't think this argument can be settled by anything other than your own taste.

It's true that for every bag of roasted coffee beans you buy from a coffee shop, a few pennies might find its way back to the original coffee farmers. But that oversimplifies the process because there are a lot of extra costs along the way. The farmer grows and harvests the coffee, but that coffee must be processed. In some areas water is too scarce of a resource to use it for wet processing, forcing the growers to dry the coffee cherries in the sun in order to separate them from their seeds (the coffee bean), and these dry processed beans sell for about half the price of wet processed. To put it another way, people that are too poor to afford wells or the facilities to clean the available water are growing coffee for a living and that coffee is priced 50 percent below the rest of the market because they can't spare the water for the processing. Lack of WATER, for the love of God, reduces their profits by 50 percent.[25]

From there, the coffee beans make their way to an importer/exporter, either via middlemen or directly. By the time they get to this level, your beans are likely under the stewardship of a big faceless multinational conglomerate or else a government itself. This is the level at which the International Coffee Organization operates. The flaw in the system is that the government officials involved may be pocketing the extra funds rather than making sure they get to the farmers that need it.

We're still not at the end of the line. From here the beans are sold to actual coffee companies. Think Starbucks, Folgers, etc. These companies then need to take care of the final tasks of distribution and processing (roasting) the beans. Next, the processed and packaged beans make their way to supermarkets and coffee shops and, finally, into your cup.

Your coffee goes through a lot of steps in its journey from farm to cup and there are a lot of people involved in facilitating that journey. And you better believe every one of those people gets their piece of the pie. The fact is, the poor coffee farmer is a pretty small actor in a big economic machine. But they're probably also the only ones that have to make decisions about which child gets to have an education while the other one gets sent away to work in order to pay for it.

This inequity in the system has spurred various methods to combat it. For our purposes, though, speaking very generally, we can say that the more direct the route from farm to your cup, the better. Thus, the flatter we can make this whole process, the better it is for consumers and, in a very indirect way, for the farmers as well.

Making coffee at home with beans ordered over the Internet is a good start. It makes things cheaper for you and it cuts out a few of those extra steps. Roasting your own coffee is even better. With the money you save by buying green coffee beans, it's way easier to buy organic, so you can make your coffee knowing that the poor farmer probably didn't contract strange illnesses from pesticides used on your coffee.

You also have the option of buying "Free Trade" beans, which are certainly controversial in their own right. When the system works, poor cooperatives can, sometimes with the help of micro-loans and other economic help facilitated by the fair trade coffee buyers, afford community building projects like water wells, schools and coffee processing facilities. Unfortunately it doesn't always work well, as some of the farm coops are corrupt and the extra money never makes it back down the chain to the farmers. But in those locations, the conventional coffee market can be even more corrupt and farmers are held in perpetual poverty by banks increasing fees and interest rates to ensure that the loans are never paid back.

Some critics say that FT beans don't really get the farmers very much more money compared to the inflated price you'll pay for the roasted beans at the end of the line. The free trade system certainly has issues, but no moreso than the regular market and at least it tries to guarantee a little more money to the people that need it most. Also, you can cut off some of this inflation by only buying green coffee and roasting it yourself. In other words, if you think it's weird that your neighborhood cafe sells roasted FT coffee beans for $20 a pound, but their other beans are in the ballpark of $15, it's a fair bet that the extra five bucks is not all going to the farmer. This gouging can be somewhat stemmed by buying green coffee beans for home roasting simply because it removes at least one, or possibly two, of the more inflated steps.

Yet another effort, called "direct trade," means that a coffee shop or roaster can buy their beans directly from the source. Direct Trade is not without its own difficulties, as outlined in a blog posting by an independent roaster called "Direct Trade Sucks."[26] It is more likely that a group of roasters and coffee shops join together in a co-op like Dean's Beans[27] before undertaking this sort of effort.

Summary

The global coffee trade is not a perfect system, but improvements are being made to try and get more of the profits to the people that need it the most. And we can all help in very real, actionable ways, while enjoying our coffee more than ever. As of this writing, Fair Trade certified farmers are supposed to receive $1.55[28] per pound of coffee compared with the 80 cents non fair trade farmers get on average.[29] So take this into account when you're buying coffee beans and just don't buy it if the place is charging an exorbitant amount for the FT beans. Even if you don't end up buying FT, organic, shade—grown, etc, the fact that you are learning about the industry is likely to change your habits somewhat. While I recognize that all of the above strategies have their trade-offs, my position is that participating in the FT/organic/shade—grown economy can be a form of market signaling that shows the coffee industry (they watch the statistics very carefully) that consumers want to support socially responsible coffee, which encourages further changes across the coffee industry. Making more of your own coffee at home helps to flatten this whole process and shorten the number of hands involved. I highly encourage people to experiment with home roasting, which may be the biggest way to individually impact how much money you're spending on coffee per month and the footprint your personal coffee habit has on the world.

The coffee industry is innovative and there are smart people working hard to make the trade more environmentally friendly and economically equitable. By the time you are reading this book, there may be new innovations in economics, engineering or infrastructure that helps secure micro-loans for clean water, innovate coffee processing or make distribution more efficient. It's possible to enjoy an amazing cup of coffee, knowing exactly where it comes from, with a smile on your face because you may be helping children born into poverty secure an education, medical treatment and a future.

Barista's Dilemma

Here's the big secret that the coffee bourgeoisie doesn't want you to know: when you make the decision to open a for-profit coffee shop, you have no choice but to sacrifice quality in order to make money. Personally, it takes me about 10 minutes to make one cup of my home-brew, and I can pretty confidently say it's better than the drip coffee in 90 percent of the coffee shops out there. However, if I try and open a coffee shop and sell coffee using the exact same method, I'll only be able to serve six customers per hour, which would actually be an exhausting pace.

I can tell you from personal experience that after making the third cup in a row, you start looking for ways to make the process more efficient, which necessitates cutting corners.

30

How much time do you think the two overworked baristas in this Incheon, South Korea airport coffee shop are able to spend on quality control for each coffee served?

The only way you could really make this whole process worth your time would be charging well over five bucks for a cup of black drip coffee. That's not a price point most consumers are willing to pay, especially since most people don't really know the difference between the black coffee at the local diner and the same from Starbucks (putting aside all the problems people have with Starbucks, the "Coffee of the Day," brewed in huge batches, is still better than diner coffee).

Making things cheap and efficient is a requirement of getting into the cafe business. Unfortunately, there's no way to do that without sacrificing at least some taste.

Some specialty coffee shops with extensively trained baristas undoubtedly serve truly excellent coffee that blows my coffee out of the water. But the prices at these places would blow your mind as well. I highly recommend trying these places when you find them, and to strike up conversations with the baristas about their methods and their beans. The baristas at these places look at making coffee as an art form and, for the most part, will eagerly engage customers in conversations about the finer points of extraction.

Cafes like this are always limited in terms of space and labor, but making profit isn't their top priority. They view themselves as artisans bringing their passion to the masses. These are not the coffee shops that aspire to become corporate behemoths, simply because they know that they can't maintain quality control while opening branches in every country of the world. The ones that do aim for world domination have different priorities that are not in line with quality control. They know they're not going to serve you the greatest cup of coffee you've ever had in your life, so they're just going to ruthlessly add sugar, chocolate, and whipped cream and hope you don't think too much about the basic flavor of the drink, or your expanding waist line.

All us coffee lovers out there owe Starbucks a debt of gratitude. To this day, Starbucks is the only coffee shop within five miles or so of my parents' house in Missouri, and it wasn't that long ago that I was on a long solo drive through West Virginia and finding a Starbucks was a godsend. We can't all be privileged enough to live in a megalopolis with a thriving artisan coffee scene, so I don't have a lot of patience for the haters.

Still, there is a lot to appreciate in good coffee other than marveling at the amount of chocolate syrup and whipped cream that can be crammed into a liter-sized bucket. If we were to create a metaphor comparing coffee shops to food, then we can say the artisan cafes are akin to a high-end restaurant employing a thoroughly trained chef while the neighborhood Starbucks is more like a fast food burger joint. If you live in a small town with very few restaurants at all (like the town I currently live in), a fast food burger is a rare treat that is thoroughly enjoyable for what it is, even though you might make a damn fine steak at home.

Coffee Myths

Coffee has a PR problem and it doesn't have its own PR firm so there's a lot of misconceptions out there about it. I'm not just talking about the old wive's tales about it stunting your growth or yellowing your teeth (kinda true, actually). Here we'll go through just a few of the most common myths surrounding coffee and determine what is what.

Does espresso have more caffeine than coffee?

Well, yes, if you are comparing milligrams of caffeine per volume of liquid. However, a serving (cup) of coffee is much larger than a serving of espresso, so if you are talking about milligrams of caffeine per *serving* of liquid, then a cup of coffee can have anywhere from two-three times the amount of caffeine as a single serving of espresso.

So if you're at a coffee shop and trying to decide what gets you the most caffeine for a minimal investment, probably some version of a red eye; drip coffee with one or two (or three or four) extra shots of espresso added. Usually extra shots are 50 cents or so, so this is a fairly economical way of getting a caffeine boost.

Is coffee unhealthy?

First of all, I'm not a doctor, so if this is a serious concern of yours, you should really do your own research and consult with a real doctor. My answer to this question though is: *it depends.*

Your particular physiological makeup might make you more sensitive to caffeine, while your college roommate had no problem downing four cups of coffee just before bed. Some people even claim that coffee makes them tired and puts them to sleep. So the effects of coffee varies a lot between people.

Just for the sake of getting a bird's eye view on the debate about the relative healthiness of coffee, let's take a look at Wikipedia's current list of coffee-related health risks:

- Caffeine dependency
- Cancer (19 of the 1,000 chemicals in coffee are known carcinogens for rats, but also occur naturally and not necessarily linked to cancer in humans)
- Gastrointestinal problems
- Anxiety and sleep changes
- Cholesterol
- Blood pressure
- Effects on pregnancy
- Iron deficiency anemia
- Coronary artery disease

Contrast that list with the list of possible **benefits** of coffee:

- Reduced risk of Alzheimer's disease and Dementia
- Reduced risk of gallstone disease
- Reduced risk of Parkinson's disease
- Cognitive performance
- Analgesic property
- Antidiabetic
- Liver protection
- Cancer prevention [sic] (linked or possibly linked

to preventing oral, esophageal, breast, endometrial, prostate and pharyngeal cancer)
- Cardioprotective
- Laxative/diuretic
- Antioxidant
- Prevention of dental caries
- Gout
- Blood pressure

Just going by these lists it seems that the benefits outweigh the risks. Recent research seems to confirm that regular coffee drinkers have a lower risk of death (whatever that means. I'm pretty sure the risk of death is still 100 percent for all of us). But if you are prone to insomnia and sensitive to caffeine, then coffee may not be good for you. Every person is different and the jury is far from out, although the research is starting to point in the healthy direction.

I always store my pre-ground beans in the freezer because my sister-in-law's ex boyfriend's uncle was a barista for a summer in college and that's what he said to do.

No to all of the above. First of all, stop buying pre-ground coffee beans immediately. We'll talk about that in the next chapter. As for storing beans in the freezer: Extreme cold is very bad for the beans. It causes them to dry out and lose flavor. Furthermore, consider for a minute that coffee grounds can be used as an air freshener because they have a strong fragrance and also absorb other smells. I don't know about you, but I am not enthusiastic about tasting Monday's leftover tuna casserole in my coffee.

Here is what you need to know: Air tight container, in a cool (as in, room temperature or slightly cooler), dry place. Oh, and I almost forgot: shielded from light. Light can negatively impact the beans as well.

You can surmise from this that it's probably not a good idea to buy beans from giant clear plastic bins of beans that distribute the oldest beans first, after they've been sitting there for who knows how long exposed to 24-hour-a-day light in a non-air-tight container, intermingling with the leftover stale oils and fragrances from whatever beans were last in the bin that has never been washed. Yeah, I feel somewhat strongly about the way coffee beans are treated in grocery stores and even some coffee shops.

Now, if you buy five pounds of beans for dirt cheap while on a trip through South America, there's probably no way you'll get through all those beans before they go stale. In this case, it's sort of okay to put the beans in the freezer. Once you take a bag out and open it, though, do not put it back in the freezer. You've gotta use it up pretty quickly.

I only drink premium hazelnut-infused coffee. How are flavored coffees made?

I don't spend much time discussing infused coffee in this book because it is not considered premium coffee. If you must know, The infusion process involves spraying a "carrier oil" on the roasted coffee beans that facilitates the absorption of the flavor, which is sprayed next.[31]

If infused coffee is your passion, it's probably far easier to buy the same pre-infused beans that you've been buying, but you can still apply all of the same principles in *The Coffeeist Manifesto* such as roast level, roasting date, and grind.

If you really go all out and decide to DIY all the way with home roasting, but you still want your flavored coffee, my advice would be to buy two or three flavored syrups to simply add a squirt or two of flavor at the end of the whole process. Still, I hope you at least give single origin coffees, properly prepared, a chance.

Four Keys to Killer Coffee

Now it is time to go down the rabbit hole and discuss where coffee beans come from and the process they go through to get into your cup.

This chapter is all about the four critical elements of amazing coffee. They are:

1. Beans
2. Roast
3. Grind

4. Brew

Simple right?

Beans

Bean selection is not something that you will have a lot of say over except in choosing what company you buy your beans from. One aspect of beans that you DO have a lot of choice over, though, is choosing a blend or a single origin coffee. You also need to make sure you're buying exclusively Arabica beans.

Don't get confused by the wide variety of names and labels attached to coffee beans. There are only really two species of coffee bean out there. Coffea Arabica and Coffea canephora (A.K.A. Coffea Robusta). While a Robusto cigar might be a perfectly good choice for an evening of indulgence, coffee made of robusta beans ought never touch your lips, especially in the coffee you make at home. Robusta beans are pretty much only used as "filler" beans in coffee blends to save money on the vastly superior arabica beans. And since so many people have been socially conditioned to believe that coffee is naturally horrible and must be doused with milk and sugar to be tolerable, the companies that do this can actually make a profit.

For quick reference, here are the acceptable uses for robusta beans:

1. Instant coffee. In fact, a huge percentage of the

world's robusta beans goes to instant coffee.

2. As part of an espresso blend ('blends' will be explained soon). Some roasters use robusta beans in their blends because it enhances the crema (the top layer of an espresso), which espresso aficionados value greatly. These blends are likely to be balanced specifically for espresso, making them less desirable to be used to make regular drip coffee.

3. Gas station coffee. If I'm buying coffee at a gas station instead of making it at home or dropping by a coffee shop, I'm not planning on slowly sipping it and enjoying the subtle flavors. No, I'm looking for rocket fuel and I have no expectation that it tastes like anything else.

So the first step is making sure that your coffee bean source only uses arabica beans. In general this shouldn't be a problem. Any coffee shop that halfway knows what it is doing and is not outright trying to cheat its customers will not have robusta beans. It would be like Martin Scorsese trying to film a movie using his computer's webcam. Sure, it could be done, and he might even be able to make it watchable, but why would he waste his time on such frivolous endeavors?

I did once happen upon a cafe in Seoul, South Korea proudly advertising its sharply discounted premium robusta hand drip Jamaica Blue Mountain coffee at 50 percent of the price of other places. This was in the famous Gangnam area of Seoul, known as the "Beverly Hills of Korea." Anyone that puts "premium" and "robusta" in the same sentence sentence doesn't deserve to be in the coffee business.

In retrospect, I totally should have tried both of them back to back to try and pinpoint the differences, but the fact is that anyone that is not only slipping robusta beans into their stock but *proudly* advertising it like it is something special, can't really be trusted not to have cut corners in all of the other key areas of important coffee.

The point is, you need to be aware of the difference between robusta and arabica so that you don't get ripped off, but it's not worth giving robusta any sort of serious consideration.

The first real choice you are likely to be faced with when choosing a coffee is going to be a *blend* versus *single origin*. The difference between these two options is exactly the same as the difference between blended whiskey and single malt whiskey. Almost every roaster has their own proprietary blends that they think are awesomer than their rivals' blends.

Just like there are people that love Johnny Walker Blue but wouldn't touch an 18 year old MacCallan and vice versa, so goes the preferences among coffee drinkers when it comes to blends versus single origins.

I have to confess that I myself, coming to coffee after some education in the worlds of the wine, then scotch, connoisseurs, have gravitated almost solely towards the single origins. I have just recently started branching out and trying a couple blends of respected local roasters whenever I travel.

The point is, there are many, many, many different flavors out there. If you're wondering what the difference is between the arabica bean grown in the soil of Indonesia and the arabica bean grown in the soil of Honduras, the short answer is: nothing. The long answer is: the dirt, micro-climates, bugs, etc. Coffee, just like wine and cigars, connects us to the earth and the labor of the farmers that watched over their fields that we might enjoy the fruits of their labor. Literally.

Thinking about all that, isn't it kind of a waste to just mindlessly chug your 32—ounce ice coffee diluted with milk, chocolate syrup, and whipped cream?

There is a lot of coffee out there marketed as specialty coffee having succulent flavors such as chocolate, hazelnut, cinnamon, or vanilla. This is *infused* coffee. The beans themselves are the same as any other beans, but have gone through a process to infuse them with extra flavor.

The final spin in terms of types of beans is the "peaberry." The peaberry is genetically no different from any other coffee bean. Without getting into the mind-numbingly boring specifics, I'll put it like this: just as a minority of people are born left-handed while most of us are born right-handed, there is a small percentage of coffee beans that come to maturity at a smaller than others. These are separated and called peaberry. For some reason, peaberries are more common in coffee from certain areas, such as Tanzania, and they do have a different taste due to their slightly different development. Does this mean peaberry beans are better than normal beans? Only if you personally think they are.

"Washed" beans have been separated from their fruit by a relatively new process that is not quite standardized. You might see variations such as "machine" or "semi" washed. I can already sense your eyes glazing over, so I won't get into further detail. This brings us back to the most important question: Does it affect taste? The answer on this one seems to be yes, but while there's difference in the taste, which one is better is, yet again, up to you. All processing methods can produce high quality coffee if done right. High quality, but different nuances.

Anyway, the point is that there is no right or wrong way to pick a coffee bean. I do, however, believe that you should know what you're spending your hard earned money on.

It is understandable that you wouldn't know what you're buying though, the way some coffee chains give their coffee beans misleading names. I don't think it is intentional. Here's what I'm talking about: several roasters sell proprietary blends of beans labeled "espresso roast." Buying these beans and going home and putting them in your French press does not mean you are drinking espresso. Those espresso beans are just plain old coffee beans. They are probably just a dark roasted proprietary blend that someone somewhere thought made pretty good espresso. You can make normal coffee with those beans just fine, but you're not drinking espresso.

Similarly, there's no rule that says you *must* use someone else's proprietary espresso blend to make espresso in your home espresso maker. You don't even HAVE to use a dark roast. It's just widely accepted that dark roasts (around the roast level called "Full City+") make better espresso. Which says to me that it's probably worth trying espresso made with a light roast just to see if conventional wisdom is up to par.

We'll get into what exactly espresso is in another chapter. For now, I'll just use all of the above as a nice segue into roast.

Roast

Similar to choosing your bean, there is no right or wrong answer in terms of dark or light roast coffee beans. That being said, most Americans have probably never tried a light roast, sampled within a few days of roasting.

Before we get into that discussion, it's important we talk about the issue of freshness, because it is one of the two most important keys for making good coffee at home, and the easiest, most basic thing you can do today to drastically improve the quality of your joe.

When it comes to coffee, the stamped expiration date is almost completely irrelevant. What is very relevant is the roasting date.

Roasting is really just cooking. And when we cook anything, we are breaking down its structural integrity. In the case of a hard seed (which, by the way, is what a coffee bean really is, as the seed of a berry), this means that all of the little cracks opening up in the surface are starting to let out the internal oils and gasses.

Those oils and gasses are what you're going to want to extract and drink later. After three weeks, a coffee bean is seriously depleted of its God-given deliciousness-giving potential. After the fourth week, hardcore coffee snobs will throw it in the trash or grind it up and use it as an air freshener in the bottom of an ash tray.

Personally, in a pinch, I'll buy beans that are a couple weeks old, but I'll try and drink it in a week or two. Or three... in a pinch.

Of everything else in this book, getting fresh roasted coffee beans is probably going to be the hardest part. Unfortunately, it is also probably the most important.

The last time I was back home in the Kansas City area, I knew that the local grocery stores usually stocked beans from The Roasterie, a very good local micro-roaster. So when I went to the store to buy beans, I ended up taking all of the bags off of the shelves to find just two bags of coffee beans that had been roasted within a few weeks.

Fortunately, there are highly reputable (in fact, some of the most reputable in the world) roasters selling fresh roasted beans online. Many of these sellers only roast on certain days, so you might have to wait a week or so before receiving your order, but it will be with it. You can check out the following for starters:

- Blue Bottle Coffee
- Intelligentsia
- Counterculture
- Stumptown

Roasting your own beans is a viable option as well. It can be done on a very small scale with little more than a fry pan or wok and a wooden spoon. The beans produce a lot of smoke and "chaff" that are sure to irritate roommates, significant others and family members, to say nothing of the smell. I personally like the smell, but it smells nothing at all like what you think of when you think of the smell of coffee. Think more along the lines of popping popcorn.

You'll also need to choose a roasting level. As I said before, there is no real wrong decision here. However, considering that our culture has indoctrinated us into thinking that "real" coffee is dark and bitter, I highly encourage you to expand your horizons by leaning towards the medium and light roasts.

For the caffeine junkies out there, lighter roasts actually have more caffeine than dark roasts (caffeine, along with the more subtle flavors, gets burned up in longer roasting times).

Furthermore, based on my own personal experience with roasting, lighter roasts require a lot more skill and knowledge than darker roasts to produce consistently. This experience makes me highly suspicious of any corporation selling me dark roasted coffee and touting the superiority of the deep, rich flavors of dark roasted coffee.

Anyway, the point is that a light roast, roasted by a roaster that really knows what they're doing, is probably pretty new to you, so why not start there?

Dark roasts are considered bold and robust coffees (cheap dark roasted blends may even include robusta beans. Be suspicious of any bag of coffee that claims to be dark roasted, but has a name that implies higher caffeine content than other blends), but they have a larger margin of error. Roasters that don't really know what they're doing and corporate coffee companies like the dark roasts because quality control is much easier. Then they use their marketing to fool us all into thinking that dark roasts are the pure essence of the bean or something like that. Really it's not. It is as much the essence of the bean as burnt toast brings out the essence of the bread. Sure, you can drink coffee made from beans roasted black and shiny, but you'll be holding yourself back from a big world of subtle flavors.

When it comes to choosing a roast, here is all the vocabulary you need, listed from lightest roasting level to darkest: Half City, Cinnamon, City, City+, Full City, Full City+, Vienna (Light French), Full French.

My suggestion is to try them all.

Grind

The issue of grind is tied with roast freshness for being the easiest thing you can do to immediately improve the quality of the coffee you drink and serve. We grind the coffee in order to let out all of those succulent oils and fragrances and extract them into our cup. If you're buying pre-ground coffee, you are essentially setting those flavors free long before you're even thinking about sitting down to brew coffee.

Even if the grounds are packaged in some sort of silvery bag with a freshness-sealing doohicky, you're better off just grinding at home immediately before brewing. There are electric blade coffee grinders that are less that twenty bucks and, while not ideal, are far better than buying your beans pre-ground. Or you could cut to the chase and go ahead and spring for a burr grinder. Good ones cost from two hundred bucks and up, but I was able to find mine on Amazon.com for less than a hundred and it has served me very well over the years.

The difference between blade and burr grinders is actually pretty big and as your palate develops you will almost certainly want to upgrade to a burr grinder, but for now a blade grinder will be okay. If and when you choose to upgrade, you can convert it to (or hand it down to someone as) a spice grinder. Just remember that once a blade grinder has been used to grind fresh spices, its days as a coffee grinder are over.

Another good option is a hand-crank burr grinder. I have the Hario Slim Grinder myself and I have gotten a lot of use out of it. It takes a few minutes of elbow-grease, but it's not too time consuming and very portable. However, if you're making coffee for guests or your whole family, it is not feasible.

The most important thing about grind, far more important than choosing a burr or blade grinder, is that you convert from buying pre-ground beans to grinding just before brewing.

Brew

There is no one single end-all-be-all of brew methods. They all have their strengths and weaknesses and it really is just a matter of your personal taste. There are far too many brew methods for me to go through all of them, but I'll highlight the ones that I usually recommend. It's important to know that there is no such thing as a "best" method of brewing coffee. In fact, the choice of brew method is probably the least important stage in this whole process in terms of ensuring you end up with a great cup of joe.

What I mean is that if I were to be offered two cups of coffee, one made with an expensive, complicated, siphon brew system but using six—months—old, pre—ground coffee beans, and the other made with a cheap

Wal-Mart drip brewer, using proper dosage and technique, I would much rather drink the coffee made by the Wal-Mart brewer but with fresh beans.

That being said, this is also where you, the consumer, have the most decisions to make and is the focus of chapter two.

Home Roasting

You know why there isn't much information out there about roasting coffee? Because it's freakin' *easy*. People invested in the coffee industry don't want you to know just how easy it is to roast your own beans. Try it a couple times and it will become part of your regular routine like washing the dishes and walking the dog.

There is no reason at all to be intimidated by the idea of home roasting. Trust me, you can do this. And when you try it, you're going to be surprised at how easy it was. You might not delve deeply into the hobby, but at least you can say you've tried it and learned a little more about the bean.

If you've found a local coffee roaster that you like, you've probably seen something like this being shown off in a window:

*Gee, who's that handsome devil half-cropped out of the picture? *Photo credit: Hwasuk Kim*

Judging by that scary-looking behemoth, you might expect coffee roasting to cost thousands of dollars before even getting started. You'd be right if you were opening up your own shop and selling the beans commercially. But for 99.9 percent of us, something like this will work just fine:

This is my home roaster, an IMEX CR-100. The IMEX roaster uses hot air to heat up and agitate the beans (agitation is important because it helps you roast every bean in the batch to a similar level). You can do the same exact thing with an air popcorn popper that you can probably find at a thrift store or garage sale for a few bucks.

For that matter, you can even do it over a stove with a fry pan or, better, a wok. This isn't really ideal for people that do a lot of roasting because the process unleashes a large amount of smoke, but for testing the waters it's just fine. A popcorn popper with an extension cord is mobile enough to take outside to the deck or porch, but it's hard to move the kitchen stove out to the backyard or garage.

So why should you try home roasting? Well, here are a few of the benefits:

- Saving big money, so you can afford to try organic, fair trade and shade grown variations
- Unique and cheap gift for your friends and family
- Learning even more about coffee
- The satisfaction of taking more control of the process
- Ensure the freshness of your coffee beans

Once you have the hardware taken care of, you need to source the software. That is, green coffee beans. SweetMarias.com is the best source I know of stateside, but there are many out there that you can surely find via your Internet search engine of choice. You'll probably need to buy the beans in bulk, but don't even worry about it because they should last a long time (we're talking years, unless they're in a flood or something else that you'd imagine would ruin a seed of any kind). Plus, they're very cheap.

With everything in place, you can start experimenting. Here are some guidelines:

- ALWAYS supervise each roast in its entirety. This is more important than just not burning the beans. One by-product of roasting is the outer skin (chaff) of the beans comes off. This chaff is flammable. Combine that with the high temperatures involved and you're looking at a potential fire hazard if you don't pay close attention.
- It's important that the beans are agitated constantly for the duration of the roast and the cooling process. This helps to ensure that all of your beans are roasted to a similar level. If you're using a stovetop method, constant stirring with a wooden spoon is advisable. If you're using an IMEX or hot air popcorn popper, too many beans will mean there won't be much agitation and you'll get a lot of inconsistency (and possibly a fire if the heating mechanism or exhaust gets clogged).
- You'll need to listen carefully for what's called "first crack." This is literally the cracking of the

bean and it sounds a bit like popcorn popping. After first crack, you can stop the process at any time and have a complete roast. It's up to you to let it go longer for a darker roast, or cut it short for a lighter roast. Not all of the beans will achieve first crack simultaneously, so you'll be listening for what sounds exactly like popcorn popping. As soon as the popping slows, you can turn off the heat.

- After you turn off your roaster, the bean is **still cooking**. You need to cool it off as quickly as possible. The ideal setup would be some kind of mesh metal pan or bowl with a fan blowing on it, but you can make do by swirling the beans around in a metal mixing bowl.

- It's very helpful to keep notes on each batch that you roast, but keep in mind that there are many variables (in particular, ambient temperature) that will cause variables in roast times.

- Something to keep in mind: a kilogram of green coffee beans is not equal to a kilogram of roasted coffee beans. You lose about 20 percent of weight in the roasting process, but you also gain a similar amount in volume. It's not entirely unlike making popcorn.

- Just like a fine steak, coffee beans need time to rest after being roasted. About 24 hours is a widely accepted guideline, but I find that the beans get even better around 48 hours following the roast.

Just in case you're skipping around in the book, and missed it in the last chapter here is a list of the coffee industry's generally accepted roasting levels:

- Half City
- Cinnamon
- City
- City+
- Full City
- Full City+
- Vienna (Light French)

- Full French

For experimenting with home roasting, I
encourage you to just shoot for "light," "medium," and
"dark" roasting levels for now. Once you have several
roasts under your belt and you can get good a good
consistent level (all of the beans the same color) within
the batch, then you can start aiming for specific roast
levels.

Doesn't sound that hard, right? It's really not.
Now, it's true that once you start getting into it it's easy
to get deeper and deeper. For example, you might find
that you have a preference for Guatemala Antigua coffee,
which leads you on an obsessive quest to find the perfect
roast level for that particular bean. And then once you
find it, every time you roast you'll be trying to replicate
it, which is easier said than done. If you open your own
cafe and buy a professional-grade roaster, you are again
increasing the level of difficulty and complexity. But
fundamentally, for those of us roasting for one week at a
time, roasting is a very simple process that you can
experiment with for very little upfront cost, but huge
savings potential in the long run.

CHAPTER TWO

Brew Methods

Zen and the Art of Brewing Coffee

When it comes to coffee enjoyment, the ritual of preparing it brings as much pleasure as the final product itself: getting everything in place, grinding the beans and enjoying the aromas freed into the air, pouring the water and watching the grounds submerge, stirring the concoction and watching the top change colors as the "bloom" (a luscious light brown-colored top layer produced by escaping carbon dioxide that usually signifies you're doing a good job) surfaces.

Of course the particular aspects of the ritual you

come to love vary with the method, but it's still its own form of meditation. It's one part of the day where all of your focus and concentration is on the process, in order to enjoy the highest quality final product as possible.

And then, the very act of appreciating it, necessarily destroys it. It ceases to exist until the next day when the whole process starts again. It doesn't get anymore zen than that.

So as I delve into the intricacies of a select group of brew methods, know that the point is not being a slave to the details, but the enjoyment of the coffee. As you have probably guessed by now, I'm a fan of experimentation, so if you skip a step, don't just throw out the whole batch. At least try it and take note of how it tastes.

I'm going to walk through a few brewing methods in a way that lets you choose how far down the rabbit hole you'd like to go. We'll start off with a discussion of the most basic coffee you can get: Instant coffee plus a couple weird methods for making very good coffee that you probably won't have to buy anything new for; you'll just need to rummage through your kitchen cabinets and draws to find the stuff. From here I'll address tweaks you can make to to that coffee pot you've already got to get the most out of it.

Then we'll address the French press, which is most people's first step to upgrading their coffee game. It takes more than just the device to get the most out of it though, and I'll tell you what you need to know.

Next we'll get to the device that I personally use

day in and day out (I have no financial stake in the company, I swear). It's not a thousand dollar espresso machine; rather, it is fashioned out of high quality, but inexpensive, plastic that can stand up to the heat of near boiling water.

After that, I'll discuss why many people misunderstand the pour over method as the easiest way of making premium coffee. I'll explain the steps you need to follow to really get the most out of it.

After I tell you about the fanciest, and perhaps most expensive, of all these methods, the vacuum pot, we'll talk about some regional coffee brewing methods, and then wrap things up with trendy brewing methods you might be seeing around town lately.

Instant Coffee: Beggars CAN be Choosers
Just what is instant coffee anyway?

For a startling number of people it is what comes to mind when they think of coffee. Indeed, the market for instant coffee is massive and it is probably the only reason Coffeea Robusta still exists. My own mother-in-law, God bless her, went out and bought me a jar of expensive imported instant coffee after she heard from my wife that I love coffee.

Outside North America, in fact, there are places

where instant coffee is the norm and it is available in single-serving 'coffee sticks' made up of powdered milk, the coffee, and a generous amount of sugar. In the case of Korea, this is a remnant of the Korean War, where United Nations forces, accustomed to freeze-dried coffee due to their Meals Ready to Eat (MRE) packs, shared the brew with locals. The Nestle corporation is one of the biggest players in this modern international drug delivery cabal, although most of us in North America would associate the corporation more with hot cocoa than with coffee.

Instant coffee is produced by a freeze-dry process that starts with brewed (as opposed to being made from the coffee beans directly) coffee. This process preserves most of the caffeine content, but much of the subtlety of a cup of coffee escapes, leaving behind a bitter, shallow, one-dimensional flavor.

Now do not get me wrong. I am not judgmental about instant coffee. In fact, one day (a few weeks before the birth of my second child), I was in the grocery store with my family and stumbled upon a deal on bulk instant coffee packaged with a pretty nice little Moleskin-type notebook. I snatched it up in anticipation of the sleepless nights I was expecting in the near future.

The reason this particular brand caught my attention though is that it represents a new method of making instant coffee that companies are experimenting with; mixing a traditional freeze-dried coffee with coffee beans ground to an extremely fine grind. While it still does not produce what I consider "good" coffee, as a drug delivery system for staving off Monday morning zombie symptoms, it does represent a significant improvement over traditional instant coffee.

It is also worth noting that if you enjoy the coffee drink 'Irish coffee,' which is a mix of coffee, whiskey (although some people use Irish cream), and whipped cream, you'll only get the authentic version by using, you guessed it: instant coffee.

Additionally, when it comes to cooking with coffee, imparting a savory coffee flavor can be tricky. Adding regularly brewed coffee in enough of a quantity to get a good taste without adding so much liquid as to change the dynamic of the mixture is, in my experience, impossible. Espresso shots deliver slightly better results, if you're closely following a recipe by someone that knows what they're doing in the kitchen. Instant coffee seems to add that distinct 'coffee-ness' in a satisfactory fashion. I suppose it makes sense that, since you're using the coffee to merely accentuate the final product rather than enjoy the various distinct characteristics of a particular varietal, that using the freeze dried essence of that coffee (or even just coffee grounds) would work out better.

There is an important lesson to draw from this chapter on instant coffee that underscores the entire purpose of this book: "Good coffee," as in specialty/third wave single origin coffee, is not automatically "better" just because it was made by someone with a handlebar mustache. You have to consider what the purpose the coffee you are purchasing is going to be. As a general rule, the more things you're going to be mixing with the coffee, the less you'll be able to enjoy, or even notice at all, the unique aspects of that coffee. The thing I hate about coffee snobbery is the implication that if I reach for a package of instant coffee at six o'clock in the morning because I know using my grinder will wake up the baby, I am somehow an uncivilized barbarian. As much as I love a cup of expertly hand-brewed direct trade coffee from an artisan roaster, in that moment where I have to figure out how to manage my morning commute on a few hours of sleep, I just need the darn coffee. I would snort it if I could.

Cowboy Coffee: An Enjoyable Cup Totally Off the Grid

We will be starting our tour through various coffee brewing methods with a (very) short chapter on the most basic brew method that I've ever run across. I know it as 'cowboy coffee,' but you may have heard it referred to as 'camp coffee' or some other variation. There is a method of making coffee on a fire using a type of coffee pot known as a percolator, but cowboy coffee is even more basic than that. Here's the recipe:

1. Boil water in a pot

2. Add coffee, coarse ground (2 Tbsp /cup)
3. Wait until the grinds settle on the bottom
4. Ladle it out (or dip your cup in) and enjoy

The recipe works almost as well for single-serving cups as it does for a group of people. You may find it works slightly better for making a larger amount of coffee though, because the larger pot will give the grounds more room to settle, allowing you to skim more ground-free coffee off the top. It should also stay warmer while you wait for the grounds to settle. Some people claim that if you add a few drops of cold water, it helps the settling process, but this hasn't worked for me when I've tried it.

I wanted to include cowboy coffee in this second edition of the book for a couple reasons. The first is to underscore that coffee, at its heart, is a pretty simple thing that doesn't require special expertise. Even this basic recipe can be upgraded by substituting recently ground, fresh roasted beans (over the can coffee that is typically used). In fact, I would put money on fresh beans, freshly ground, and brewed via the cowboy method being much tastier than old beans, ground several weeks ago, being brewed by the fanciest siphon pot chemistry set you can buy.

In other words, if you would permit me the indulgence of christening a 'law' of brewing coffee at home, this would be it:

Bean freshness trumps brew method.

If you remember nothing else from this entire book, this simple guideline will serve you well.

Cold Brew: Cheap, Easy, and Delicious.

"Ice coffee" and "cold brew" coffee are in fact two different things, although they are not mutually exclusive. Cold brew coffee is a method of brewing coffee that does not require high temperature. In fact, you don't necessarily even need water any colder than room temperature for it to be considered cold brew coffee.

Cold brew is made using a cold process, but can be served hot, cold, or anything in between (cold is recommended though). Iced coffee can be made by any particular method, but is served on ice.

What coffee shops serve as iced coffee is usually a particularly weak americano made by pouring espresso over ice, then filling the cup the rest of the way up with water (ensuring as the ice melts that it becomes even more watered down). This produces a cup of iced coffee, or as I like to call it, mild espresso-flavored cold water. It has to be extra-watered down because that's the only way to tolerate the bitter, all body, taste with no flavor clarity.

If you take your iced coffees with an extra shot or two, it will get the job done and at least it's a coffee-related drink you can tolerate on a hot summer day. But why pay money to a coffee shop for a mediocre product that the most anyone can really say about it is that it's drinkable?

Here's the deal: you can make a legit iced coffee, with serious flavor clarity and very little body (most people dislike 'body' saying it's too strong), made through a cold brew process in the comfort of your home. The total brew time is 12-24 hours, but it takes about 10 minutes of actual work on your part to make, and the only equipment you need, most of us have sitting in the back of a kitchen cupboard somewhere (and if you don't, it won't cost more than a few bucks to procure).

In addition, if you're not quite ready to make the psychological leap into grinding your beans fresh every time you brew, this will be a nice gentle way to start experimenting with your coffee. When you buy your beans (freshly roasted from a quality roaster I'm assuming...), just ask them to grind it just a little finer than for drip coffee, or, a little finer than "medium-grind." You don't need a large quantity either. A pound is way too much. You need closer to ¼ of a pound, or, about a full cup. Most places probably won't sell you a single cup of their roasted coffee, but I'm willing to bet you could talk most of them into selling you a half pound. If you're at a roaster serious about their coffee, just tell them your spouse doesn't like coffee and it would take you 6 months to finish a full pound and they'll probably rush to help out a fellow coffee-phile in need.

With that half pound, I'd simply suggest making two batches of cold brew.

So here's your shopping/treasure hunt list:

- 2 large (quart size should do it) glass jars
- Some kind of filter (I like cheesecloth, but some kind of metal mesh, or even a large paper coffee filter, can be worked with)

Instructions:

1. Buy freshly roasted, fresh ground coffee (if you're going single origin, I like Central American coffees for cold brew).
2. Pour 100 grams/¼ pound/1 cup of coffee (there's some flexibility here, You don't need to be exact) into one of the glass jars.
3. Fill jar with room temperature or cooler water

(filtered water is highly recommended, even if your tap water is perfectly drinkable. This is because of minerals that may be safe to drink but still offset the taste of coffee).

4. Stir.
5. Put lid on jar.
6. Put jar somewhere dark and cool (a refrigerator works great, but a cabinet should do just fine).
7. Wait 16-24 hours (the shortest I've waited was 18 hours. I usually try to do a full 24).
8. Filter the coffee. This shouldn't be too hard as many of the grounds have probably settled in the bottom of the jar. If you're using cheesecloth, double it up and cut out about a square foot's worth. Place it over the top of the empty jar, and slowly pour the coffee through the filter.

Ready for brewing

Brewing for 16-24 hours

I recommend filtering twice

A week's worth of coffee

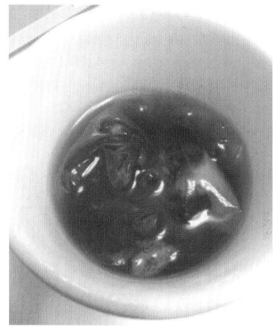

Yum!

You might need to empty the filter and start again. Just throw away the grounds clogging in the filter and keep going.

Clean out the first jar (don't put a big mass of coffee grounds down the drain. Spoon them into the trash, or save them in some kind of receptacle to use as an air freshener). Rinse it out, and filter again, back into the original, now clean (but not with soap) jar.

What you now have a cold brew *concentrate* that should be good for about 7-10 days. When you want some, all you have to do is pour some into a cup, and add cold water at about a 2:1 water to concentrate ratio, or whatever ratio you like better (I like 1:1, but most people won't). You might be surprised at the sweetness you taste without adding the squirts of syrup that you use at the coffee shop to make it palatable. In fact, the cold brewed coffee you just made is better than any iced coffee or ice americano you could get anywhere except at the highest-level coffee shops.

From here there are some variations to try. They're all super easy:

- Dilute with hot water, or heat in microwave, for hot coffee.
- Dilute the concentrate with cold milk instead of water.
- Use as an ingredient in a chocolate protein-based smoothie for coffee flavor and caffeine boost. You can come up with some healthy frozen concoctions that would cost a fortune at a franchise coffee shop.
- Freeze the brew in an ice cube tray. Use the cubes to cool down your usually too-hot-to-drink morning brew (I'd put them in a big zipper bag to keep other flavors from your freezer from getting into the coffee though).
- Whatever else you can think of to try. I encourage you to experiment often and widely.

In addition, there's the ever-so-slightly more complicated hot-cold brew method. I first read about this method on an online site where a serious scientific discussion was going on about whether or not cold water is really capable of pulling out much of the gas, oils, and solubles (presumably including the precious caffeine) from the coffee grounds. A compromise method was suggested that calls for hot water, about the same temperature used for regular methods, which is to say, about 95 degrees celsius.

This method allows the coffee to briefly bloom, in theory pulling out more of those lovely solubles, before filling the jar the rest of the way up with cold water. This allows one to get more of a balance between body and flavor quality out of their cold brew.

This method is nearly identical to the first, but with a couple extra minor steps:

1. Buy freshly roasted, fresh ground coffee.
2. Pour 100 grams / ¼ pound / 1 cup of coffee into one of the glass jars.
3. Pour about 200 grams (two cups) of *near* boiling water (boil it, then wait 30 seconds to a minute) into the jar. Stir it as best you can. It will be pretty thick, don't worry about it.
4. Fill jar the rest of the way with *cold* water (I recommend cold water for this rather than room temperature in order to cool down the concoction faster).
5. Stir
6. Put lid on jar.
7. Put jar somewhere dark and cool.

8. Wait 12-24 hours.
9. Filter the coffee.

Enjoying the coffee is exactly the same.

Is this method *really* better than the other one? Well, in my opinion, yes. I offered the first method simply to show the simplest way possible to do it. It won't produce a final product that everyone will love. Just remember that it's not intended to be consumed straight and really needs to be watered down a bitIn my opinion, the second method produces a final product that is better balanced and will appeal to a wider range of people. It will still need to be diluted with water. But both are worth trying.

Percolator Pot: The way Grandma Used to Make it

Coffee percolators are relatively foolproof and offer a step-up from cowboy coffee in the sense that you're not going to be chewing your coffee as much. Percolators aren't highly recommended if you're trying to improve your knowledge of and taste for coffee, but the very strong brew they produce is largely seen as acceptable for making coffee for a large amount of people in an easy and convenient way, especially for camping. Taking a look at the strengths and weaknesses of percolator pots can teach us some important principles about brewing coffee in general though.

Again, the 'bean freshness trumps brew method' guideline applies. If you have some nice beans on your hands and only a percolator to brew it with, well, you'll be able to produce a very drinkable cup of coffee out of it.

Percolators have a tendency towards over-extraction largely because the water temperature is much higher (boiling, usually) than in other methods. What this translates to is that bitter flavor coffee has become so closely associated with.

The principle at work in a percolator is that hot water will rise up into the pan holding the course ground coffee, wash over the grounds, and drip back down into the main reservoir of water as it cools. This process is then repeated many times until the brew is at a desired strength.

Theoretically, with practice, you could improve the end product by keeping a sharp eye on temperature control. Try to make sure the water doesn't come to a boil (keep the heat low). This will likely require a longer brew time, but, again, the same water being washed over the same grounds repeatedly can also lead to an over-extraction, even if the water temperature is in check.

The principle behind the percolator is also used with the large coffee 'urns' that are often employed to brew coffee for very large groups of people.

The lesson here is in the fine balance between water temperature and steep time. This balance is difficult to achieve with a percolator pot, but should be in the front of your mind as you move forward in your exploration of fine coffee. As you evaluate a brew method, be thinking about how difficult it will be to manage those two factors along with your own tolerance for dealing with complicated machinery, price, and a messy cleanup.

Using What You've Got: The Standard Coffee Maker

My faithful drip coffee maker has lasted around six years and is going strong. I paid a little more for it at the outset, but it has a couple qualities (gold filter, insulated carafe) that really paid off when I started to really learn about making coffee:

Just because someone has some fancy, expensive new coffee-making contraption does not mean that person knows how to use it properly. Your idiot cousin that just got back from a year in Japan and brought with him a contraption that looks like a science fair project probably believes that the fact that he spent a hundred bucks on the thing and that it looks cool and complicated automatically means it makes better coffee.

Well, it *can* make better coffee, if you know what you're doing. As impressive as it is that he was smart enough to figure out how to get it on an airplane without security thinking he had a bomb in his suitcase, if he can't explain why it makes better coffee, he probably doesn't know how to get the most out of it.

That's an extreme example, but people, including myself, I admit, love to brag about their fancy coffee brewing methods. I have one of those ridiculous contraptions (called a vacuum or siphon pot) and can count on one hand the number of times I've actually used it. There are far easier ways to make coffee just as good, although different.

I don't recommend that anybody rush out and start spending big money on whatever coffee contraption is trendy at the moment if you're not serious about taking the time to learn how to get the most out of it. In fact, that coffee maker you already have is probably capable of making very decent coffee if you follow these essential tips:

1. Fresh roasted, fresh ground coffee. You'll get sick of me saying this by the end of the book, but that's just how important it is.
2. Proper dose. Most people use way too little coffee, out of the mistaken belief that less coffee grounds = a less bitter, weaker cup of coffee. This means the grounds are over-extracted and, well... bitter. For

most methods of making coffee, about 2 "coffee scoops" (1 coffee scoop is about 2 level Tablespoons) of coffee grounds for every cup of coffee you intend to brew is recommended. A standard cup of coffee is considered to be 8 ounces... so most of us are probably brewing double cups.

3. Experiment with your filter. I'd recommend a reusable gold filter. It's better for the environment and doesn't add dust and other particulates from the paper filters that have been in your cabinet for a decade. Some people like the paper filters though. And still others use paper filters soaked in hot water first. The Aeropress, my personal favorite method for the past couple years, which I'll talk about in more detail later, uses a small paper filter, and I have good results with soaking it in hot water.

4. The only thing other than fresh roasted beans that I'm going to tell you to run out and buy is an insulated carafe. The real problem with most coffee makers is the hot plate with a glass carafe that continues to cook the coffee after it's finished brewing. This is very bad for your coffee. Either get an insulated carafe, or make sure to turn off the coffee maker AS SOON AS it's finished brewing and pour the coffee out of the carafe and into some kind of insulated container to keep it warm.

5. Built-in grinders are nice, but in most cases they are blade grinders. Blade grinders are inferior to burr grinders and usually not worth the extra price attached to them if you could just buy a separate grinder for cheaper. Still, I have had one of these for years that makes very decent coffee. I keep it in my office for use when I have a group of people visiting and feel like I need to be a good host by making coffee. If you can find one with good reviews on sale, I say go for it.

If you don't have an insulated carafe, then go buy one

If you read through this whole book and decide that other methods of brewing coffee are just too much trouble, but you would like to get a new coffee maker that can make good coffee, pay special attention to tips 3 and 4, as there are very good, albeit pricey, options on the market addressing these very issues and they'll make very decent coffee out of the box. With fresh roasted beans and the proper grind, of course.

Press Pot: The Old Stand-by for Good Reason

The first step many people take when they decide they'd like to try to upgrade the coffee they make at home is to buy a fancy-looking 'french press.' Actually it's a fine choice. Also known as a 'press pot', it is capable of making some damn good coffee. However, there are a lot of mistakes that people make with the press pots that means they're not getting the quality product they should be. We'll get to that, but first let's go over the basic brew method:

1. As always, get freshly roasted, freshly ground beans.
2. Standard 2 "coffee scoops" of coffee grounds for every cup of coffee you intend to brew (a standard cup of coffee is considered to be 8 ounces... so most of us are probably brewing double cups).
3. Pour the appropriate amount of water into the press for its size, the amount of grounds you have, and the amount you intend to brew.
4. Put the top on, but do not press the plunger yet.
5. For a weaker cup, let steep 3.5 to 4 minutes. For a stronger cup, 4 to 6 minutes.
6. SLOWLY press the plunger to the bottom of the pot.
7. Pour coffee.

Okay, that's the basics. I'm going to talk about several possible tweaks you can do to improve this process, but there's one thing I want you to promise me right here and now to never do:

- Pour a first cup, slowly sip away at it while leaving the brew in the press pot, then pour the second cup later.

The only problem with press pots is that they're usually hard to clean and are made out of glass and break easily.

That coffee in the bottom of the press pot never stopped steeping. It's been in there for ten, twenty, or thirty minutes. You're better off pouring it into a thermos mug to keep it warm rather than let it stay in the pot.

Some of you are realizing right now that you just spent big bucks on an ingenious "travel brewer" that combines a thermos coffee mug and a press pot. You're wondering if you wasted your money, right?

Well, you didn't waste your money. The thermos

press pot does offer a slight improvement over other press pots in that the water stays hotter through the brewing process, allowing for a more thorough extraction. I encourage you to use it in this way and *only* in this way. Do not use it to make a quick cup of coffee and also to drink that coffee on your way to work. This device should be used as a press pot only, not as a coffee mug. After pressing the coffee, you need to pour the brew out into a separate receptacle for consumption.

With that out of the way, we can get into some tweaks that will take your press pot coffee to the next level.

- Before you even get started, warm up the French press and, especially, all the metal components with hot water. As metal is a natural heat conductor, putting a cold plunger into hot slurry can inadvertently bring down the temperature during the critical steeping stage.

- While steeping, do not place the lid/plunger on top. Instead, use a porcelain disk to cover the top. Before you press, take two spoons and in one fluid motion, scoop off the top layer of coffee grounds. Don't worry about getting all of the grounds, it's impossible, but this makes a big impact on the taste of the coffee.

- Some people recommend stirring the slurry after pouring in all the water, some don't.

Try both ways and determine your own preference.

- Whatever coffee brewing method you use, I highly recommend heating your mug ahead of time with hot water. This helps the coffee to maintain its temperature longer, as well as enhancing the whole sensory experience of it.

- If you screw up and forget about the coffee you had in the press and it's been ten minutes, there's a failsafe that will help rescue any cup of coffee no matter how bad and it will still be better than a typical franchise cup: Bailey's!

The Aeropress: Easy, Clean, and Makes Great Coffee

If you're wanting to try something new, get online and order yourself an Aeropress. Unless there's some special reason that makes an Aeropress impractical, it's the device I find myself recommending to people over and over again.

My Aeropress is a critical component of my travel coffee set up that goes with me whenever I'm on the road.

The company that makes the Aeropress (Aerobie) stumbled upon an amazing idea. Judging from the cheap packaging of their product and ridiculous marketing claims (that it can make any kind of coffee including espresso, which is just flat out WRONG), it seems like they either a) Created the thing completely by accident and don't realize the quality of their product, or b) Are intentionally trying to make it look bad because they know how awesome it is and want to protect its cult-like following.

Well, okay, they probably are just trying to appeal to as many people as possible, but I promise you if I had seen the box before buying it, I would have given it a pass. The sales copy sounds like something right out of a late night infomercial.

All that aside, the Aeropress is an amazing

contraption.

The basic idea is not so different from a press pot. The coffee grounds are fully submerged in the water for the duration of the steep time before being pressed through a filter. Somehow the way it is pressed directly into the cup, though, makes all the difference. The flavor profile comes out similar to a press pot, though possibly with more flavor clarity and slightly less body.

The big benefit the Aeropress has over a press pot is in how easy it is to clean. Take the lid off, continue pushing the plunger until the little puck of coffee grounds and filter falls into the trash. Rinse with water. Done.

There are various methods of brewing with the Aeropress that are easy to find online, but the one thing everyone agrees with is that the instruction sheet included in the packaging is useless. Most recommended methods seem to be some variation of the "upside-down" method:

1. Insert the plunger into position (in line with the number "4" on the side) as per the accompanied instructions.

2. Turn the Aeropress upside down and let it rest on a flat, stable surface such as a kitchen table or counter top. It will remain in the upside-down position until the very end.

3. Pour the freshly roasted, fresh ground coffee into the chamber, 1 generous scoop for every cup you intend to make (don't pay attention to the

measurement markings on the Aeropress).

4. Pour hot water in the 185-200 degree range into the chamber and stir.

5. Steep for 2 minutes.

6. Some people recommend an additional stir halfway through the steep time. Others wait until the very end. I've experimented with both and can't tell the difference, frankly.

7. Soak one of the included paper filters in hot water (convenient if you're already heating up your mug), place in the lid and attach to the top.

8. Empty the water out of your now warm coffee mug and place upside down on the top of the Aeropress.

9. Flip the mug and Aeropress right side-up together. Or you can just put the coffee mug on the counter/table like normal and only flip the Aeropress. This was messier for me though.

10. Gently press the plunger. Stop as soon as you start to hear the hiss of air going through the filter.

When I first started with the Aeropress I added hot water. This would make about two full cups of coffee in standard coffee mugs. I'm at the point now where I just drink it straight. It's really up to you.

Pour Over: The Choice of Dedicated Aficionados

Pour over (or, "hand drip") coffee may be the least intimidating first step into fine coffee. The setup is cheap and it appears to be as simple as can be. All of that is true; however, the simplicity of it is deceiving. In fact, it is one of the most difficult methods to master due to the rapid loss of water temperature as the stream of water slowly leaves the kettle and filters through the coffee grounds.

Depending on how you look at it, this could actually be a strong point. If you're pretty sure that you're going to stick with it and really try to master the art of making coffee with the pour over method, the time you put in to experimenting and studying it will pay off. But let's not overcomplicate things. Fundamentally all you need to do is run the hot water through the coffee grounds, then a filter, and into a cup. Yes, it might take some work to get your pour over skills on par with the pros, but even the cups of coffee you enjoy along the way that don't measure up are still probably going to be better than the coffee you might have gotten at a diner or gas station.

To get things started, you'll need your dripper, filters, a coffee mug, a kettle of hot water (about 200 degrees fahrenheit. So yeah, having a thermometer handy isn't a bad idea either), coffee mug and, finally, some fresh and finely ground, recently roasted coffee beans. Don't run out and spend big money on a fancy drip coffee setup.

A pretty typical—looking ceramic dripper

Coffeegeek.com, a very reliable source for all things coffee, advocates using a cloth filter for pourover coffee.[32] Their method seems to be much more forgiving in terms of technique, but it's a more expensive setup. It all depends on you. I have not personally had the pleasure of trying the cloth filter for pourover, but if I happened across one I would certainly try it.

With all that out of the way, we'll move on to the basic instructions:

1) Most pros won't put the dripper directly over the coffee cup. They'll use a small pitcher as a receptacle. This is really your call. Whatever you're putting the dripper on top of, do it now.

2) Put the filter in place and fill with coffee grounds. I recommend starting with about 17 grams of coffee grounds and experimenting from there.

3) Pour the hot water through the coffee grounds. This is where all of the skill and technique comes in, but don't even worry about that the first couple times you do it. Just get the water through the grounds and into the cup. As time goes by, start experimenting. First, you just want to moisten the coffee grounds. Think of this as priming them for the extraction. Then, as you pour, make sure you evenly distribute the pour. Professional baristas will do this in a spiral motion around the coffee grounds. It would surely be helpful to watch a few YouTube videos for tips as well.

4) At the end, after removing the dripper, some people think that adding a little splash of hot water opens up the flavor. I don't agree, but try it both ways and see what suits you.

Once you've got the basic technique down, you can then move on to the Chemex, which uses the same principles, but is capable of making larger quantities of coffee. In fact, the Chemex is probably the best way to make awesome coffee if you have a group of people over.

Another option is the "Clever" coffee dripper, which is a patented, variation on the pour over method that prevents the water from filtering all the way down. This addresses the primary problem with the hand drip method, which is loss of water temperature, meaning that it would probably produce a more forgiving, more consistent cup pretty close in flavor profile to that of the Aeropress. The Clever is a very worthy, inexpensive, option.

Vacuum Pot: The Cool Factor

The Siphon/Vacuum pot is the ultimate show-off coffee brewer. Looking exactly like a chemistry set, complete with an open flame, you might feel intimidated when first approaching the setup. Although the intimidation is somewhat justified, experimenting with a vacuum pot can pay off both in the cool factor of it and in the unique flavor profile you'll enjoy over other methods.

First of all, it's not a bad idea to get a vacuum pot with a larger capacity. Frankly, you're not likely to use your vacuum pot to make your morning zombie coffee. You'll need your wits about you to monitor the open flame and get the timing right. Most of the time you'll be using your vacuum pot to make coffee for company, which is appropriate considering the crisp, clean flavor profile you'll get which will surprise most guests.

It's also a good idea to swap out the little oil lamp that probably came with your vacuum pot. It's usable, but it will take forever to let the heat build. Considering the importance of timing, you don't want to be sitting there waiting on the thing to heat up. It's recommended to swap it out for something like this:

There are a lot of different techniques for brewing with a vacuum pot and experimentation is critical, but the basic method goes something like this:

1) Fill the reservoir up to the guideline with hot filtered water.
2) Place the stem of the chamber loosely into the opening, leaning to one side so it doesn't seal.
3) When the water starts to boil, straighten the chamber and allow it to seal.
4) Water will begin to move up the stem

immediately, so be ready with your coffee grounds.

5) When almost half of the water has moved into the top chamber, dump the finely ground (8 grams per cup of coffee) coffee grounds in the top and stir.

6) Continue stirring gently as the rest of the water rises into the chamber.

7) This is the hard part: As soon as all of the water is in the top chamber, turn down the heat on the burner. There is a fine line between too hot (the water in the chamber is visibly boiling) and too low (the half-brewed coffee starts to come back through the stem, into the bottom reservoir, too early).

8) Let steep (keeping the heat constant) for 65-80 seconds.

9) Remove the heat source and turn it off. This will create a vacuum in the bottom reservoir, pulling the coffee through the filter, stem and into the reservoir.

10) There will be some bubbles as the last of the coffee filters into the reservoir. This means it's finished.

11) Very gently remove the top chamber and set it aside. Pour the coffee into the mugs and enjoy!

34

It's a complicated process but the second or third time you do it you'll start to get the hang of it. You need to fully clean everything after every brew, but you can re-use the cloth filters many many times.

You'll also want to do plenty of experimentation with shorter and longer brew times to find your own personal sweet spot. While the method I described here will certainly get you started, there are a lot of variations you can find online using your favorite Internet search engine that can help you branch out and perfect your technique.

Regional Variations: The Way Mom Used to Make it

Coffee had been around for centuries before the rise of specialty coffee. As its consumption spread across the world, people all along the way were trying various ways of enjoying it. Thankfully we finally figure out which types of coffee plant produce the best coffee and have perfected roasting techniques.

Those innovations are relatively recent arrivals, though. As coffee wound its path across the face of the earth, it made its mark in various cultures where a distinctive local method of preparation developed. You may well have grown up with a specific method of making coffee that reminds of you of home every time you drink it.

The specialty coffee world does not spend much time with these methods and recipes for enjoying coffee. Probably because they were developed at a time when the quality of the beans available were pretty low, these regional varieties of coffee usually involve dosing with heavy amounts of sugar and/or milk to make it palatable and suit local tastes.

The coffee bourgeois would likely say this 'ruins a perfectly good cup of coffee,' because their perspective is all about bringing out the unique characteristics of each coffee bean, but this misses the point entirely.

If you grew up drinking one of these types of coffee, you have got nothing to feel bad about from enjoying coffee the way Mom used to make it. But do not let that stop you from going deeper into the world of coffee either. There is a whole new level of enjoyment you can dive into, and you can always come back home to your beloved Turkish, Vietnamese, or Cuban-style coffee.

Considering Turkey is one of the first places the enjoyment of coffee spread to from Africa, it is only natural the nation has its own way to enjoy the brew. Turkish coffee is actually quite similar to cowboy coffee, although a special pot is typically used to make it. It is essentially brewed by mixing near-boiling water with coffee grounds, and allowing the grounds to settle in the bottom of the cup. When I have had it prepared for me, it has always been served with a generous amount of sugar already added, but this is not always the case.

Looking back on my own history with coffee, a friend, recently returned from a trip to Vietnam, making me a cup of Vietnamese coffee was probably a turning point in my own development as a coffee enthusiast. I had never heard of it before, and I was so impressed with it that I rushed out and got my first French press soon after. Vietnamese coffee at its essence is coffee served with a generous (1/4 to 1/2 of the serving glass) amount of sweetened condensed milk. Most of the time the coffee is brewed with a french press, the milk stirred in, and then iced. This method will always have a special place in my heart because of that memory, which I suppose highlights the most important aspect of all of these methods.

Our third example, Cuban coffee, is the only method of the three that is based on espresso. In fact, sometimes it is called "Cuban espresso," although most people use a stovetop espresso maker which, as you'll learn shortly, is not authentic espresso (but still enjoyable). The way Cuban coffee was originally prepared was with an espresso machine, and by adding the sugar directly on top of the coffee grounds in the basket before pulling the shot. The home variation of this usually involves putting a bit of sugar in the bottom of the cup to start, and just pouring off a tiny bit of the coffee into the sugar and then stirring to make a creamy paste. The rest of the coffee is then poured into the cup, but the paste will rise to the top, effectively simulating the crema of an espresso, but with added sugary deliciousness.

If you find yourself traveling to one of the above destination famous for its coffee, don't look down your nose at the people preparing it by dumping in a load of extras. Think of it as a precious opportunity that the locals have taken it upon themselves to share the way they have had coffee their entire lives with you.

There are certainly more regional specialties when it comes to methods for making coffee, so this is not an exhaustive list. In this rare case I actually do not recommend trying to make them at home if you have never had them before. Save these for when you get a chance to have the real deal. It will be yet another opportunity for coffee to bring people together, facilitate conversation, and make the world a better place.

A Word on Trendy Coffee Brewers

Since the publication of the first edition of this book, it seems like links to every shiny new coffee brewing contraption ends up, one way or another, in my inbox. Also in that time, coffee pods have taken the world by storm. Although I am generally supportive of the ideas of experimentation and breaking new ground in the world of coffee, I would caution my readers from throwing too much of their hard-earned money at the latest cool new video proposal on some crowdfunding site, or on a device dependent on any kind of 'pod' for financial, culinary, and ethical reasons.

At the end of the day, that newly proposed device you're so excited about backing is unproven and, thus, risky for people on a budget to invest in. Yes, it may be designed by a team of engineers, and they may have put a lot of work into it. They may even be passionate about coffee to boot, but I have seen many such devices turn out to be unreliable and flimsy, aside from being outright gimmicky.

Coffee pods, meanwhile, when you do the math about the cost per cup, are generally THE most expensive way to consume coffee beans. For the money you're spending on beans that are stale and pre-ground, you could be getting some of the best beans in the world directly from some of the greatest roasters in the world at a fraction of the price.

It is also important to remember that most of what you see on crowdfunding sites are built by new startups preaching some type of innovative brew method which means that, by definition, there are no trustworthy reviews yet. The enthusiastic dreamers behind the product are no doubt sincere in their belief about the amazing taste of the coffee produced by their device, but what do industry experts have to say about it? What about the ones with no direct connection to the device or its makers? These are the voices that need to weigh in before investing your hard earned money on it.

No matter what the marketing says about coffee pods, they are incapable of producing a cup of coffee on par with what you would get using a quality grinder immediately before brewing fresh roasted beans, using any of the methods from this chapter. Yes, they are extremely convenient (nearly on par with instant coffee in terms of convenience), and considering that, the coffee isn't bad, but it will never stand up to the scrutiny of the specialty coffee world. If you are reading this book, you are probably about more than just convenience. You are probably looking to expand your horizons in your coffee appreciation. For the same money you would spend on a fancy pod coffee brewer, you could get yourself a very decent electric ceramic burr grinder that, paired with one of the inexpensive brew methods already mentioned, will blow your mind.

One final point about these crowd funded launches of new coffee machines is that they may not have ways to handle refunds and returns if you just do not like the product.

Ethical concerns, while relatively minimal with crowd funded coffee brewers, are probably the largest strike against pod coffee brew systems. The environmental impact of these brewers are substantial (it takes a LOT of plastic for a single cup of coffee), and some of the tactics the pod coffee makers have taken to try to force consumers into purchasing coffee pods made by the machine manufacturers (Digital Rights Management, or, 'DRM') are, in my opinion, deplorable.

DRM is a big issue within the topic of copyright and digital technology, but I can summarize it pretty simply: Do you actually own the device you paid money for like you would a car or a book, or do you 'license' it like you would a computer software program? In general, large corporations would prefer to define consumers as 'users' that have merely licensed their products rather than 'customers' that have 'purchased' them.

Merely a semantic difference? Perhaps in the world of fifteen years ago, before computer technology was being introduced into our cars and home appliances. Consider the Indiana farmer that sued John Deere because according to his 'licensing agreement' when he bought his tractor he was prohibited from trying to fix any problem in the software of his tractor. John Deere believed they had the right to demand that he call their service department and wait for someone to drive out to his rural location and diagnose the problem. The farmer, on the other hand, believed that he should be able figure it out on his own rather than lose a crop to an incoming storm because he was waiting on John Deere tech support.

How does this apply to your coffee? Coffee pod producers, with the addition of a cheap, lightweight RFID chip on the lids of their pods, and a simple scanning device built into the brew system believe the users of their products should be forced into only using approved coffee pods in the same way that Apple prevents you from installing apps on your iPhone from anywhere else but their proprietary App Store. It's true that, for the consumers, there is a slight guarantee of quality and compatibility that being locked into such an ecosystem brings. But that slight benefit comes with an ugly (and getting uglier) downside that is starting to change the very meaning of the word 'ownership.'

Yes, this entire essay is my personal opinion. I know that saving money, saving the earth, or getting the best cup of coffee you have ever had in your life is not alway the top priority, so I'm not judgmental about people that get excited about a fancy coffee pod brew system they received as a gift (like my own brother, tisk tisk...). I've even partaken in a cup or seven made from one of these systems. All I ask is that you go in with your eyes open and make fully informed decisions about how you vote with your dollars.

CHAPTER THREE

Espresso

A Word About Espresso

Up to this point, we haven't discussed lattes, cappuccinos, frappuccinos, or for that matter, red eyes, depth charges, americanos, and so on and so on. Well, here's why: they are espresso drinks. While making gourmet coffee in your own kitchen is completely doable, with espresso it's a little tricky. In fact true espresso connoisseurs are going to have to spend at least $1000 all in (espresso maker + high quality burr grinder) to get the best at-home espresso.

As the point of this book is to educate coffee

novices as to how they can get started enjoying gourmet coffee without spending a fortune, I didn't even plan to discuss espresso at all because of these limitations. I finally decided, though, that it is worth discussing so long as people have realistic expectations.

As for me, I can get a drinkable espresso out of my setup that cost me about $300. This doesn't get me even close to the level of a trained barista on a high quality espresso machine, but it's certainly good enough to impress friends or enjoy an affogato (a scoop of vanilla ice cream with an espresso poured over the top) on a hot summer afternoon.

We'll get back to actually making the espresso soon, but let's take a look at what exactly espresso is, and why it's so hard to make. First of all, let's start off with what it is *not*:

It is not "expresso."

Well, okay, technically it is spelled expresso in Spain. But as espresso originated in Italy, it's safe to assume that most people pronouncing and writing it as expresso that they're not doing it intentionally.

Because of the confusing name, which sounds a lot like "express," people make a lot of assumptions about what espresso is. It is not just coffee made quickly and it is not just an 'extraction', as *all* types of coffee are, in fact, extractions.

Perhaps most importantly, it does not have more caffeine than regular coffee. If you compare one shot of espresso to one shot of drip coffee, yes, there is more caffeine. However, most of us drink much more than a shot when we enjoy drip coffee, and in fact, a single serving of coffee (widely accepted to be 8 ounces), has about double the amount of caffeine as a single shot.

So for those of you that don't particularly enjoy the taste of espresso (and if you've only had it prepared at a franchise or chain coffee shop, I couldn't blame you), but order it anyway to help get you through an all-nighter, do yourself a favor and stop choking it down. Just drink regular coffee.

Serious caffeine junkies probably know all about the "red eye," AKA, "depth charge," which is essentially a cup of drip coffee with one or more extra shots of espresso in it. I have no argument with this drink and have ordered it myself on occasion (it's also cost effective, as extra shots are commonly about 50 cents or so). This also works with ordering ice americanos, which I have been known to do in the summer. In fact I pretty much always order ice americanos with at least one extra shot, pretty much on principle.

With that out of the way, we can get into what espresso *is*, and why it is so expensive to make. Simply, espresso is nothing more than a method of extraction that forces very hot water through ground coffee at high pressure. It sounds simple, but the mechanism used to generate that high pressure and to supply it consistently, for the entire duration of the shot being pulled, is hard to get right with any kind of consistency.

In other words, creating a new espresso machine

is a complex feat of modern engineering that very smart people work on for years at a time. Frankly, when it comes to espresso makers, you can get a pretty good idea of how good the espresso is based on the price of the machine. Under $100? Forget it (although you can fake it). $100-200? Doable. $500-$1,000? There are some decent options out there.

All this means that while the methods I discussed for making superior drip coffee at home will get you as good or even better than you can get from most coffee shops, my advice on espresso just can't can't be held to the same standard. I can't teach you to change the laws of physics, unfortunately. That being said, there are a few workable options.

I'm not going to get into as much step-by-step detail on these as, generally speaking, you should follow the manufacturer's instructions for each type of machine. I will, however, briefly explain the process for each to help you decide if you'd like to buy one.

Hopefully by now it goes without saying, but like all coffee making methods, the freshness of the beans and the quality of the grinder will have a significant impact on the quality of the finished product.

Moka Pot: Not Bad for What it is

In the price range of under a hundred bucks, there are lots of choices, but only one that will get you even close to the taste of espresso. Notice how I said "the taste of espresso?" That was intentional, because it does not, in fact, make espresso. It is sold by various names, most commonly by the name "Moka Pot," but I've also seen off-brand versions sold as "stovetop espresso makers." Whatever it's called, it will look something like this:

My one-cup Moka Pot is a bit of an unusual design, and doesn't make very much coffee at all. I recommend the two cup version, which I previously owned.

Moka pots have a brilliantly simple design. Water goes into the reservoir, which goes directly over the heat. The metal filter is where the coffee grounds go, and the receptacle screws on top. As the water heats up, it goes through the coffee grounds and pours into the receiving chamber (in this case, a demitasse).

Moka pot tips:

- Use a course grind, like you'd use for a press pot. You might notice the holes in the filter are on the large side.
- Ideally, you want to pull the whole contraption off the heat *before* the last of the water has come up. The timing on this is tricky and takes practice.
- You do not need to tamp the coffee grounds in the basket like you would with espresso.

In fact, you want to make sure the grounds are not tightly packed. The proper amount of coffee grounds for a Moka Pot is however much it takes to make a mound (shaping it with a spoon is helpful) rising a little higher than the basket.

I can say that playing with a stovetop espresso maker is an enjoyable experience and it has its own aesthetic to it with the sounds it makes during the process.

The resulting coffee has a taste that's pretty close to espresso and can even have an impressive crema (similar to bloom, but in espresso it remains in the cup) of its own. I haven't experimented personally with making lattes or cappuccinos with the resulting coffee, but I don't see any reason why it couldn't be done. It won't be up to par with what you can get in a good cafe, but my guess is that, with practice, you could get pretty close.

You can probably score one of these for around $30 for a single-serving version, but the two-serving version seems to get better reviews and was also my personal favorite. There are also larger versions that, while I haven't personally had a chance to try them, seem to get mixed reviews online.

A Word on Grinders

If you are looking for something beyond moka pot coffee, we need to have a quick word about grinders.

A good friend of mine recently asked me for a recommendation for a nice espresso machine. He said his budget was in the $1,000-$1,500 range. He was just finishing up a basement renovation he was doing, and believed (correctly, I might add), that a fancy espresso machine would be the piece that really ties the room together. Before sending him some recommendations I asked what he had for a grinder. It turned out that for him, like most people, the grinder was an afterthought.

Here's the deal: A cheap espresso machine paired with an expensive grinder > an expensive espresso machine paired with a cheap grinder.

After explaining it to him, I finally convinced him he should plan on spending around half his budget on the grinder. On his budget, he'll be able to start pulling some pretty awesome shots (with practice).

Personally, I didn't start out in the world of espresso with a $1,000 budget. In fact, it was more like $100-$200. The same general principle about the importance of your grinder still applies. At the time I was using a sub-$100 Capresso Infinity burr grinder that, with an easy mod, can grind good enough for espresso. I used that grinder for years and learned a lot with it.

My espresso game got kicked up several notches, however, when I upgraded to a Rancilio Silvia espresso machine paired with a Baratza Vario grinder. I'll get to that soon enough, but I would be remiss if I didn't mention the fact that I quickly noticed a dramatic difference in taste (for the better) in all of the coffee I made.

Just remember that if you're looking at getting into the world of homemade espresso, shelling out for a quality grinder is something you have to bite the bullet and do. I know grinders aren't sexy in the way a sleek espresso machine is, but you will thank me later.

ROK Espresso: Authentic, Entry-Level Espresso

The current heir to the throne in the world of entry-level espresso machines is the ROK Espresso maker. The previous holder of this title was the MyPressi Twist, which attempted to harness the power of compressed air to get great shots, but the ongoing engineering challenges seem to have been proven to difficult and the company packed it in.

At the time I was writing the first edition, I was already aware of the ROK Espresso machine, but it was the new kid on the block and was still being put through the paces. As of this writing, however, the ROK is still going strong at the top of the pack of contenders for the crown of entry-level, authentic espresso machines for home use.

It's still going to run you in the neighborhood of $250, which isn't cheap, but about half the price of the next step up. You can also use the ROK "off grid" (without electricity; it's powered by elbow grease) so you'll still be able to have your espresso during the zombie apocalypse. Honestly, it is the only contender in this space. I'm sure someone is going to send me an email about once of those bicycle pump-inspired devices, but my experiments with them left me unimpressed (and it's a LOT of work to build up the right amount of pressure).

The ROK is powered by two levers that you grip with your hands and press down and towards each other (roughly the same motion that some corkscrews make when opening a wine bottle). There's a portafilter with a small-ish basket that the company also offers specially made tamps for.

There is a big downside to the ROK that you should probably know about. It is, after all, an espresso machine, which means the grind is critically important. If you are planning on taking it camping or for other off-grid use, this presents a special problem. Hand grinding for espresso is doable, but not practical at all, and you'll probably find yourself just opting to forgo coffee altogether rather than go through the headache of grinding the beans to a fine enough level for espresso. The company itself has produced a matching hand-crank grinder that they say works well for this purpose, but it is a relative newcomer to the scene and as of this writing is not widespread. The company literature states that a standard hand crank grinder requires from 130-190 revolutions for an appropriate espresso grind, while theirs is engineered to produce an espresso grind at less than half that number of revolutions (62 to be exact).

All in all, I'm impressed with the ROK and the niche it has carved out for itself in the marketplace. Clearly there's consumer demand for something at this price point, and the technological problems of electric machines in this range have proven to be an opportunity for some intrepid engineers out there. My hunch is that the ROK will be around for a while, but new contenders could start popping up at any time.

Rancilio Silvia: Next Level Espresso; Next Level Price

In the first edition of this book, I made no attempt to introduce readers into more expensive and higher grade home espresso machines. This was partially because of my own lack of experience in the world of espresso, but mostly because I wanted to stay focused on the idea of cheap and simple ways to improve the coffee people are making at home. My experience with the Rancilio Silvia espresso machine, as well as friends and readers that have specifically asked me to help them choose espresso machines, have led to this new chapter.

If you've read my other chapters on espresso then you've probably caught my hint that making espresso is an entirely different ballgame from brewing black coffee, and it takes substantial hardware and engineering to make it happen. In practice this means that even at the $500-$600 price point, the Rancilio Silvia represents the lower end of legit home espresso machines. And even at that price point, there's a steep learning curve.

Sure, you'll be able to pull shots right out of the box, but to really dial it in and get the most of it is a long process of trial and error to perfect your own technique as well as the proper grind, dosage, and timing. All of these variables will be different depending on the bean, the roast, and the age (ironically, beans that are too fresh will present special problems in your shots).

I'm not trying to dissuade you, I just want you to know what you're getting yourself into if you decide to take the plunge.

That all being said, I am head over heels in love with my Rancilio Silvia, and that's partially because of all of the trials and tribulations we have been through together.

Believe it or not, as expensive as the Silvia is, and as much tinkering as it requires to start pulling great shots, the Silvia falls into the "semi-automatic" category of espresso machines. "Manual" espresso machines have more direct controls for things the water pump and temperature controls, while a semi-automatic espresso machine will just have one switch because the pump and boiler come pre-programmed. That still gives you, I am assuming an amateur barista like myself, a good deal of control because it lets you time the shot to your preferences rather than cutting it off at a predetermined time (which would make it an automatic machine). Since it is going to take a great deal of experimentation, you want the freedom to be able to let that shot run for longer and shorter times as need be.

"Super-automatic" espresso machines would be what you might find at the local big box retail store on sale for around $100, boasting one-touch espresso (not real espresso, by the way — They can't generate the proper pressure). A sturdy version of this type of machine might be acceptable for an office setting where quantity is more important than quality, but I can't recommend them for home use.

For the same of the argument, I'm going to assume you've followed my advice and gone with a semi-automatic espresso machine. Now you're ready to get to work. The variables you have to learn to balance are: bean freshness, dosage, grind, tamp, and timing.

I know, I know. I've been going on and on about how you want beans as fresh as possible. I stand by that for regular coffee, but for espresso, the gasses coming off those roasted-yesterday beans are going to really throw everything off. I'd recommend starting with beans three to four days out from roasting for your experimentation.

Also, make sure you go through the whole process on a dry run a couple of times. The first time I tried using my Silvia, although I'd watched several YouTube videos on pulling espresso shots with it, I was thrown for a loop when the portafilter (the part with the handle that has the 'basket' on the end for grounds) just wouldn't attach. I nearly panicked, as everything else was ready. I'd done the temperature surf (more on that a little later), and everything else was in place.

It turned out that my particular machine is just a little idiosyncratic in the way the portafilter slides in and it just took me a few times to get it to go in place. I would have saved myself nearly the stress if I had taken the time to do a dry run.

As for dosage, it would be great if I could make a concrete recommendation for something along the lines of 18 grams of coffee grounds for a double shot or whatever, but when it comes to making espresso there is always a fair amount of spillage and you always need more than you think you're going to need. Then if, after tamping, there's too much and you end up having to do it all over again. As you can see it is really hard to measure with any accuracy.

Again, experimentation is your friend. If you are in the habit of roasting your own coffee in small batches, you might want to go ahead and buy a large amount of beans from somewhere to practice with. Learning to make espresso leads to wasting a lot of beans. If you're using beans that you've lovingly roasted yourself, you'll probably stress out over every clump of coffee grounds that ends up on the floor. Buying some beans from somewhere can save you some stress.

Getting the tamp right is similarly difficult to get right. I have it on good authority that the tamp is less important and not to be stressed about, but from personal experience I think at least a little tamp is necessary. For the tamp, I recommend pressing lighter than you think you need to at first. Too light of a tamp might not be a big deal, but too heavy can muck things up. The real problem is that tamp, like dosage are both art more than science in my experience.

Not all espresso machines will have to 'temperature surf' but the Rancilio Silvia does. Here's the issue: The Silvia has a single boiler that performs both functions of steaming milk and producing the hot water for espresso. For ideal espresso, you don't want the water to be as hot as it needs to be for steaming milk, and the Silvia will, by default, signal that it is ready for action (there's a boiler light that is on when the water temperature is being raised) at the higher threshold. You want to start pulling your shot at the moment the light clicks back on again to bring the temperature back up. You can either wait, or you can run water through the system without the portafilter in place, which will bring the temperature down. When the light clicks back on to show the boiler is heating up again, get the portafilter in place and start pulling your shot.

Finally, timing. You're aiming for something close to 25-30 seconds to pull a full shot. When you first get started, though, it's either going to trickle out at a snail's pace, or it is going to come rushing out without any resistance at all. Go ahead and taste it if you like, but be ready to start from the beginning and go through the whole process again, tweaking your dosage and tamp. And then do it again. And again. And again...

I've pulled some amazing shots with my Silvia, but I still have issues with consistency. I've noticed that when I go through an espresso phase, the shots get better and better until I turn back to preferring black coffee for a while. Then, when I go back to espresso, the cycle starts all over again. Still, I love the process and it has taken my appreciation of all forms of coffee to yet another level.

Espresso Variations

Armed with a couple relatively inexpensive choices for making home espresso, there are many ways to actually drink your espresso. Here are some of them:

Espresso*
Americano* -Espresso with water in a 1:1 ratio
Latte*
Mocha**
Cappuccino**
Espresso Macchiato**

Latte Macchiato**

Breve*

Espresso Con Panna*

Flavored Latte

Long Black* -Good for easing the transition into enjoying espresso.

Red Eye / Depth Charge* -Also good for transitioning into espresso.

Affogato* -My favorite dessert on the planet... except for maybe brownies.

* -Doable with no extra equipment purchases that have not already been mentioned

** -Requires a method of frothing/steaming milk

I'll get into greater detail on all of these in the next chapter on decoding the coffee shop menus.

CHAPTER FOUR

On Coffee Shops

Coffee Shop Appreciation

Columbia, Missouri, may be my favorite town in the world, has a lively local coffee culture.[36] Lakota,[37] my personal favorite of the downtown establishments, welcomes people to come claim a table, buy a bottomless cup of coffee, and hang out all day working on a paper or chatting with friends. I did most of my writing for grad school there.

Aside from coffee, Lakota also sells beans, teas and some locally produced baked goods. Its indie atmosphere attracts patrons of all types and everybody hangs out together in harmony.

When a Starbucks opened up down the street, and closer to the University of Missouri campus, a lot of us were worried that Lakota would be out of business soon.

If anything, as time went by, it got *harder* to find a seat.

If you've made it this far, you are more than capable of making coffee competitive with that at 95 percent of the coffee shops out there in the comfort of your own home with minimal extra investment. Plus, if you choose to, you know how to get decent espresso as well.

That all being said, there are still some very good reasons to enjoy coffee shops.

As much as I love my own coffee, there's something about the atmosphere at a coffee shop that I still love. If I've got a free afternoon I want to spend writing or devouring a great book, a coffee shop is my first choice of places to spend it. If I need a meeting spot, a coffee shop is much more conducive to a natural, relaxed conversation than an office or restaurant.

Certain coffee shops will have special brew methods that are not practical for most of us to try at home. It may be a special limited edition $50,000 espresso machine, or they might have a Clover (if they have a Clover, which makes regular coffee using a process similar in philosophy to a French press but uses some high tech automation, it really is something to get excited about and you should definitely try it).

Another great reason is to try different methods of brewing coffee that you haven't mastered yet and to try and pick up some of their techniques or to compare the taste of their coffee to yours and try to gauge how much you're learning. Beyond this, a small local roaster is a great place to buy your fresh roasted coffee beans and to sample their espresso while you're at it. I've had great conversations with baristas and coffee shop owners just by asking questions about their roasting process or their brewing methods. Whenever I move into a new area, identifying the good coffee shops and making friendships there is how I feel like I'm settling in and making myself at home. These relationships give you a friendly place to go simply to hang out, socialize, read a book, get some work done, etc. etc. It also gets you the occasional freebie.

Pro Tip: Many high end espresso machines (especially operated by baristas without substantial training) pull double shots by default. If you're friendly with the baristas and business is slow, they'll often just give you the second shot rather than pitch it.

So how do you identify a good coffee shop from a bad coffee shop? How do you know if you're getting ripped off?

Frankly, I'm willing to lower my standards a bit for a coffee shop with a good atmosphere and nice people. In fact, knowing what we now know about the time and effort it takes to make really good coffee, I am very understanding that for a coffee shop to make a profit, it needs volume. However, I do not like being ripped off. In this spirit, I've identified a series of guidelines that often signify whether a coffee shop is competent and charging reasonable prices, or if the establishment is cutting too many corners on its coffee, banking on the ignorance of its customers.

This part of the book is your coffee shop self-defense manual. After reading it, you'll know how to spot the coffee shops worth visiting from those that don't really know what they're doing or, even worse, are flat out trying to rip you off.

Coffee Shop Tourism

I often get asked for coffee shop recommendations in my town, and I always find it a hard question. On the one hand, I know the reason they are probably asking me is because they would like to experience another level of coffee from what they are used to. But on the other hand, I strongly argue that the way to get the very best coffee, outside of the top 1% of coffee shops (of which you may be hundreds of miles away from one), is by making coffee at home for yourself.

Still, at the end of the day, I'm happy to engage in

any conversation about good coffee. I'll usually ask what kind of coffee they like, what they typically use coffee shops for, and go from there.

I do love visiting coffee shops, but when I do it is as much about the experience of the coffee shop as it is about the coffee itself. I am always on the lookout for places that either make great coffee, or have a particularly enjoyable setting, or both.

On a recent vacation with my family, my wife surprised me by booking a room at a small guesthouse on what was known as "coffee street." As expected, the street was filled with coffee shops, all with great views of the beach and ocean. As I walked the street in the morning, deciding which place to enjoy my morning cup along with the book I was reading, I ended up walking right past all of the brand new buildings with various design concepts that would be equally appropriate at a night club. What caught my eye was a coffee shop that, rather than tearing down the old building and building something new and stylish, built their shop right into the dilapidated, borderline un-safe, house that originally stood on the land.

Inside, the coffee shop was the standard espresso-based fare, which disappointed me a little, but I enjoyed perusing the various indie music and homemade crafts they also sold. Then I noticed a small sign board near the register advertising their Turkish coffee. On normal occasions I'm not particularly fond of Turkish coffee, but in this unique coffee shop surrounded by probably twenty other cafes, it stood out from the crowd.

That particular cup of coffee, on that particular day, in that particular coffee shop was a diamond in the rough. The entire experience was enjoyable, although I was initially disappointment at the number of coffee shops in the area that made no effort to distinguish themselves by the quality of the coffee. Instead they opted to try to capitalize on the recent fame of the street by jumping on the bandwagon and appealing solely to the indoors-sunglasses-wearing, selfie-taking crowd.

If you're too snobby about it, the mission to find similar diamonds in the rough is full of this sort of disappointment. I do not expect every place to make award winning espresso, but I do expect to see some effort that shows they care a little bit one way or another. Offering hand drip coffee, but putting it under "Americano" on the menu (yes, I have actually seen a place calling itself a cafe do this) communicates a willingness to play to the lowest common denominator, rather than helping people on their own journeys to know and appreciate good coffee.

Say what you will about Starbucks, the place is consistent. The beans may be roasted until they are pitch black and of questionable freshness, but at least they will be ground and brewed fresh, as per company policy. The company is also not in the business of franchising which, they claim, allows them to maintain a certain level of quality across all outlets. This may bring the scorn of the specialty coffee world upon me, but when I'm on a business trip and sleep-deprived and just need a strong cup of coffee to keep me going for an important presentation, or a reliable Internet connection that I know won't cause me problems, a Starbucks is a welcome sight. On the other hand, if I'm exploring a new city and looking to get a feel for the mood of the place, it will be disappointing if all I can find is a Starbucks.

Whenever I'm visiting a new town, I've usually got an eye peeled for those possible diamonds in the rough. I don't always have the time to visit the places that I bookmark in my mental map, but I'm always taking notes.

Now I'm sure you are wondering: "Gee, how can I learn to keep my eyes peeled for those special places too?"

While a lot of the characteristics of a coffee shop that would get my attention aren't things that I can perfectly articulate, the next chapter lays out some of the general guidelines I use for evaluating places I happen to come across.

The Rules

I promised that I'd provide some guidelines for figuring out if the new coffee shop in the neighborhood is truly serving specialty coffee or if the fancy roaster on display in the window is just for show. Whether you have been patiently waiting for this chapter, or thumbing through the book searching for it, this is the chapter you have been looking for.

Rule #1: Attention to detail

This first rule is very subjective. In some cases it

may mean the interior design is immaculate, usually with a minimalist concept, and they are fully transparent with details like roasting dates and origins labeled clearly.

In other cases, the shop may be messy and disorganized, but the mad genius behind the counter has an encyclopedic knowledge of all things coffee and is clearly passionate. Both of these shops would be worth trying out in my book. How can you be sure? By asking a lot of questions.

You can get a lot of information about a coffee shop and its procedures by asking about, for example, how light they roast their beans, the flavor profile of their beans, or how they roast their beans. If the employee responds rudely or takes your question as a general intrusion, it's either a sign that they know they have something to hide from someone that knows their stuff, or that they don't even know themselves.

Rule #2: If you see the word 'robusta', give the place a pass.

Luckily, this should be pretty rare. In fact, I'm surprised I even need to mention it at all, but apparently I do, as I've seen with my own eyes coffee shops proudly boasting about their premium origin coffee, with robusta in the fine print.

It is true that, according to the intertubes
(specifically Wikipedia), Robusta beans make up about
20 percent of the world's coffee trade, but the vast
majority of these end up in instant coffee or as cheap
filler beans in some proprietary blends. They have more
caffeine, but that is to the detriment of the taste. Anyone
proudly advertising (or displaying, as in the picture
above, taken at a family-style buffet restaurant that
boasts about its fresh roasted coffee) their premium
robusta beans fully deserves to go out of business, which
they inevitably will.

I might welcome robusta in the high octane
QuikTrip brand coffee at 3am on a drive across Kansas,
but it is unacceptable if I'm paying more than a buck and
have any expectation of actually enjoying it.

Rule #3: If you are looking for a good cup of coffee rather than just a cheap caffeine boost, be leery of any place that is a coffee shop + something else (ie, beer/wine + coffee, bakery + coffee, pasta + espresso, etc, etc, etc).

Making a good cup of coffee takes time and dedication; art, if you will. It just isn't economical for a place devoted to serving quality coffee to also have to deal with the hassle of setting up beer taps, uncorking wine bottles, and checking whatever pastries are cooking in the oven. A coffee shop that tries to be more than a coffee shop is spreading itself too thin. Just be aware you're not going to get high level coffee at the places.

Most people haven't had the chance to try quality coffee. Even most coffee lovers out there take it for granted as a bitter drink to be diluted with milk and sugar. The 'Bakery Cafes' and 'Hof and Coffee' take advantage of this fact. It's not necessarily an intentional deception. In fact, they may not know the difference themselves. Fundamentally it doesn't matter to their bottom line because people don't know any better... or just don't care.

Rule #4: Avoid Americano.

As you may already know, Italians started calling watered down espresso 'americano' as a way to make fun of American G.I.'s for drinking weak espresso during World War II.

In some establishments, americano is considered 'pretty much the same' as drip coffee. Or at least it is by coffee shops that don't care about quality or their customers.

Coffee has become trendy in recent years and various businesses have seen coffee as a way to make some easy extra cash. In fact, a friend of mine that was involved in the opening of a restaurant a few years back told me that they did not even have to purchase their own espresso machine. Contracted to serve only a certain brand of coffee, the company supplied the espresso machine. As to who trained the bored high school part timers on how to use this beautifully complex marvel of modern engineering, who knows.

The point is, any restaurant, Coffee/Wine Bar, or bakery calling themselves a cafe, etc, can get a nice espresso maker at relatively low (or no) cost to them and be up and running making extra cash selling Americanos at three bucks a pop.

Good business, but most likely terrible coffee.

Rule #4a: Any sign offering a discount for takeout coffee is pretty much saying, "We'd be glad to take some pure profit from you, but don't need you around dirtying up the place."

It might actually turn out to be a drinkable espresso, but you're taking your chances.

Rule #5: If it's a caffeine buzz you're after, avoid espresso and americano entirely.

Yes, espresso is a type of coffee, but not all coffee is

espresso. Espresso is just one method of extracting flavor from coffee beans that happened to have been invented in Italy.

Espresso is produced by forcing very hot water and steam through coffee beans under high pressure. This is not something easily done and, in fact, requires high-quality, expensive machinery. I would be extremely skeptical about purchasing the $50 home espresso maker on sale at Wal-Mart. In fact, the level of engineering sophistication required to produce good espresso is even difficult at the $250 price point, although the ROK Espresso machine previously mentioned does a decent job.

The fact is, most espresso machines/grinder sets worth their salt are well over a thousand bucks for good reason. Commercial-grade espresso makers can be well north of that, into the tens of thousands of dollars range, which is why getting your espresso fix at coffee shops, rather than home, is usually preferable. But just having an espresso machine isn't good enough. It is a complicated piece of machinery and the user needs to know the subtleties of the proper amount of coffee grounds, just the right amount of force to tamp with and the proper cleaning and maintenance of the machine. It requires training and skill. Are you really sure that the aforementioned high school part timer working the espresso machine in between bussing tables at the corner sandwich shop has the proper training? Plus, espresso has only about half the caffeine of drip coffee. For all that, most places are going to charge you a couple bucks for an americano that really doesn't have that much caffeine in it and tastes horrible anyway.

If the place you are considering serves americano instead of drip coffee and any other red flags are going off, then it's a good bet they're cutting corners in the quality of the coffee. As we already established, they were probably able to get a good deal on the machine, picking it up for low to no cost, and probably cut corners in the training of their employees as well. Save your money, and head down the street to the convenience store for an energy drink or Green Tea.

Rule #6: If you're not just after a caffeine buzz, go ahead and try getting into espresso.

That all being said, there is a whole lot to appreciate about fine espresso. It may be an acquired taste, but it is well worth it. Give it a try! At the very least, try easing yourself in the direction of espresso by trying a long black. It's just americano with a little less water.

Espresso is also the base of the various mochas, lattes, frappes, etc, that we have all enjoyed on occasion, in spite of the sugary calorie-bombs that they are. Espresso is the building block of all those drinks, and there is about two calories in an espresso. At the very least, I'd recommend trying it just to see what it is that your white mocha frappuccino tastes like before it is drizzled in chocolate syrup, whipped cream, ice cream, and whatever else they put in those things.

Rule #7: Just because a coffee chain has a big name, it doesn't mean the coffee is better. In fact, depending on the neighborhood and town, it's usually the opposite.

While there are certainly legit questions to be asked about the labor practices of the big international coffee corporations and the way they treat the coffee growers, this rule is purely about the disrespect they show their own customers by using insultingly stale beans and overly dark roasts.

Once a bean has been roasted, the structural integrity of the bean is broken down and the natural oils and solubles that contributes to the taste of the bean will start to escape. The snootiest of the coffee snobs will say to throw beans out after two—three weeks. I say four. . . but I've been known to stretch that farther than I'm willing to admit publicly, and with appropriately bad results. I know those dark beans look shiny and good, but that shine is the oil, which is supposed to be on the inside of the bean, escaping.

Here's the rub: Most, if not all, big coffee chains roast their beans in their headquarters' warehouses and put them on a truck or boat to travel across the country, or even the world, meaning the coffee beans they are going to use to prepare drinks for the customers they claim to care about so much, can be six months old upon arrival. You do the math.

If they are not upfront about the freshness of their

beans, there's a reason. Drinking stale coffee isn't going to hurt you. You won't get food poison from it if you drink it a few weeks after the roasting date. So technically they can put the expiration date as some theoretical far off date. It's just a ripoff. You're not getting value for your dollar.

On my last visit to Kansas City, I went to a local supermarket to try to find beans from The Roasterie (a local microroaster I mentioned way back in Part I) and I had to pull every bag off the shelf to find ONE bag that had been roasted within four weeks. I guess there's another lesson here:

Rule #7a: Don't buy coffee beans at the grocery store.

Rule #8: All else being equal, favor coffee shops with a roaster (that is actually in use) over those that get their beans from somewhere else.

All the coffee snobs reading this book just cringed.

Yes, just because someone owns a roaster doesn't mean they know how to use it. Similarly, just because a place isn't a roastery, does not mean they do not get their beans from a highly reputable source. However, if you're looking down a random street and you have three coffee shops to choose from, one of which is a big name corporate chain, and the other two are small mom-and-pop shops, I'd probably go with the mom-and-pop shop with the roaster in the window.

While there certainly are coffee shops out there where the roaster is little more than part of the indie decor, in my experience they are usually at least competent with the roaster and the atmosphere is far better. The chances are pretty good that if they went through the trouble of buying an expensive roaster and they actually use it and keep it in good condition, then at the very least they probably *care* about what they're doing with the coffee and the cafe will be a decent place to impress a date.

Rule #9: Sometimes we all end up at Starbucks. Educate yourself about the 'hidden' menu

Ever wonder why "tall" is Starbucks version of "small"? Well, actually it's not. Allow me to introduce you to Starbucks' "short" size. If you're not interested in coffee (or if you've already had too much) and just need a place to kill an hour of time before meeting someone without spending a bunch of money, go into a Starbucks of your choice and order a short americano or coffee of the day. That is if you can't stomach espresso (which would probably be the cheapest). You'll save some money, but not feel like you're freeloading by taking up one of the comfy chairs while you wait.

Even if you already knew about the short size (it's old news for Starbucks fans), this particular tip can elevate you to coffee-snob status by ordering a short cappuccino. A cappuccino larger than 6 ounces is not, in fact, a classic cappuccino due to the difficulty in properly frothing milk in an amount above a certain volume. Besides this, the tall and short size cappuccinos have exactly the same amount of espresso in them. So unless you're just a really big fan of warm milk (which is the only thing that's added to make a tall cappuccino), there is absolutely no point in ever ordering a tall cappuccino.

Starbucks has, apparently, a whole slew of beverages available off-menu to make loyal customers feel cool, I guess. I haven't ventured too far into this territory, but I have confirmed that the short cappuccino is alive and well in Korea's Starbucks chains and, in fact, I recommend it.

So for meeting someone by a subway station or going on a coffee date, finding a Starbucks is a pretty safe bet as they are everywhere. You can actually order a short size of anything on the menu.

Rule #10: Try new things

If, after trying espresso, you find that you really like americano, great! But at least now you know why you like it, rather than just accepting the lie that americano and plain black coffee are one and the same. I'm not against people following their own tastes. In fact, what I am trying to help you do, most of all, is to find your own taste, not just blindly rely on common wisdom.

And when you do find the real deal—a truly artisan coffee shop that takes the time to explain the subtitles of the different beans and roasts—by all means try their hand drip, siphon, dutch and even a properly cold-brewed iced coffee. These places are getting easier and easier to find and each one has a style all its own. Some are trendy, some are gritty. Some have big aspirations, offering latte art classes, etc., while others focus more on their roasting and make crappy latte art, but amazing coffee. I have found almost all of them to be welcoming and happy to talk to someone interested in learning about their craft.

Decoding the Menu

Before I really got into coffee, if I got dragged into a trendy coffee shop, I'd go in with a chip on my shoulder. I'd usually end up saying, with a not-very-subtle attitude, something like, "Can I just have a normal coffee, please?" I thought of myself as a coffee purist, but I was really just ignorant of the huge variety of choices on the menu.

As long as we're on the topic of visiting coffee shops, I'd be remiss if I didn't try and help you decode the labyrinthine menus. It will probably be split into categories such as espresso drinks, food, tea and probably a separate section that I'll call "fusion" drinks. This is where you'll find the frappucinos, smoothies, juices, etc. Unless you're at a truly artisan/specialty coffee shop, classic drip coffee will be relegated to a small corner of the menu, if it's available at all. I'm going to focus specifically on the coffee, or at least coffee-based, drinks.

Ristretto

This is a shot of espresso that is cut short (less water). It makes a small but flavor-packed shot that is worth trying sometimes. Generally speaking, only order this if you are already accustomed to the acquired taste of espresso. It isn't for the faint of heart.

Americano/Long Black

I know I seemed harsh on americano in the last chapter, but I really don't have a problem with it. It's the coffee shops/restaurants passing off americano as regular coffee that I have a problem with. An americano or, even better, a "long black" (basically a strong americano) can be a great way to ease your way into the world of espresso appreciation if you can't take plain espresso at first.

Espresso Macchiato

Strictly speaking, an espresso macchiato, sometimes called a cafe macchiato, is literally just espresso with a milk "mark." These days in most cafes, they'll probably use foamed milk. The ratio should be about three parts espresso to one part milk.

Again, this is a good one for easing your way into espresso, but it's also very good in its own right.

Espresso Con Panna

The only difference between an espresso con panna and an espresso macchiato is using whipped cream instead of milk. So if you like your coffee drinks strong and sweet then this is the variation for you.

Espresso Breve

Espresso with a bit of half and half or semi-skinned milk, this is a somewhat obscure variation that you probably won't see on the menu except at the most espresso-centric espresso shops.

Red—Eye/Depth Charge

Bringing together the awesomeness of regular drip coffee with the deep richness of espresso is the red eye, A.K.A., depth charge. Most people that order one of these, however, aren't interest in the taste. This drink's primary role is as a caffeine delivery system. And, I have to say, it's a pretty cost effective one, as while an espresso is usually a couple dollars, an extra shot, on most menus, is fifty cents or a dollar.

For a long, dark period of my life, I completely abstained from caffeine except for when having a migraine headache. In fact, this is when I started to fall in love with coffee. In the midst of the horrible pain, coffee came to be, first, a simple comfort, and a few minutes later, relief, coupled with an energy boost that completely turned my day around. It was via the depth charge that I could get the highest dose of caffeine in the shortest period of time, which also served as my introduction to espresso.

Affogato

Forget coffee—flavored ice cream. An affogato is the real deal. A modest scoop of vanilla ice cream served with an espresso on the side. When you're ready to eat, pour the espresso over the top. The flavor is divine and the portion size is usually modest, making it the perfect occasional treat for those of us that are counting calories.

Cappuccino

A cappuccino is an espresso-based drink originating from Italy that includes two types of milk. The espresso is considered the first layer, which is followed by steamed milk in a 1:1 ratio and then topped with milk foam. From here different cafes and even baristas will put their own creative spins on finishing off the cappuccinos. Some will create artistic designs in the foam created entirely by their pouring technique. Others sill add sprinkles of cinnamon or chocolate shavings. It all depends.

Latte

Many cafes use the latte as the jumping off point for their proprietary variations. It's not hard to do as a latte is mostly milk. But there's an important point to keep in mind: when you hear about all the fancy variations like green tea latte, chai latte, etc, they are most likely swapping out the coffee and making a drink that isn't really even a coffee-based drink anymore.

So what is a basic latte? While an espresso

macchiato adds just a drop of milk to an espresso, a latte takes that same amount of espresso, adds a lot of steamed milk, and makes an 8-ounce drink. Also, many cafes will top it off with a layer of milk foam.

The **Latte Macchiato** is a variation on the latte that just adds the espresso to the steamed milk (rather than adding milk to espresso), letting the espresso fall down through the milk to flavor the drink. It also, due to the way the espresso and milk mixes, has a weaker coffee flavor than a latte. In addition to this, there are various flavored lattes that mix in flavored syrups. Many coffee shops pass off iced latte macchiato as simply iced lattes.

Mocha

A cafe mocha is also just another variation of a latte. It's basically a latte with chocolate syrup or cocoa powder to give a chocolate taste. The name 'mocha' by the way, originally had nothing to do with chocolate. It's just the name of the port city in Yemen that was a major coffee market (perhaps the first coffee market) from the fifteenth—seventeenth centuries.

The regional coffees coming from the region came to be known for the hint of chocolate in their flavor profiles. If anything, mocha refers to coffee first, and chocolaty flavors second.

Others

Depending on the coffee shop, this may only be the beginning. These days, coffee shops will try to appeal to a wide range of people so almost every coffee shop will have non-coffee options such as teas, juices, and smoothies. There are also fusion drinks such as the frappuccino varieties invented by Starbucks. Some are honestly not bad for what they are, but this is also the territory where coffee gets a bad rap and starts being associated with over-priced, high-calorie concoctions served in bucket-sized to go cups. Just keep in mind that the more diverse the menu, the less of a coffee shop the place really is, no matter what it may call itself. It's hard to keep serving high quality coffee if you're diversifying into smoothies, paninis, cinnamon rolls, and so on.

Other Coffee Drinks

Some coffee shops get a little frisky with the typical coffee experience and offer intriguing experimental ways to enjoy coffee. Although I am generally skeptical of coffee + X abominations, it can be fun to see what all the hype is about. The three I am going to focus on here are all a type of cross-over drink that borrow elements from the world of alcohol.

Nitro coffee is the current hot trend that seems to be sweeping cafes as well as restaurants. Nitro coffee is basically cold brew coffee that is served out of a beer tap via nitrous gas. Think of it like carbonated coffee, except the nitrous gives a smooth Guinness-like mouthfeel and other interesting traits. This has some advantages in the sense that a bar or restaurant can serve coffee "on tap" without too much trouble, presenting an interesting, non-alcoholic, option for customers or their designated drivers. It helps that nitro coffee very much looks like a stout or other dark beer, so you could enjoy it socially in a bar setting without feeling like the odd one out.

Personally, I've been unimpressed with the taste of nitrous coffee. The nitrous imparts its own flavor that I think takes away from the coffee. In other words, I'd rather just have the coffee. It is an interesting idea though, and it's worth giving a shot if it sounds like something up your alley. I think it is intended more for people that are not fans of coffee, but still like coffee-flavored things like coffee ice cream and such.

I find **hop-infused cold brew coffee** more intriguing and am currently experimenting with making it myself. The first place I heard of it was Oddly Correct, a specialty coffee shop in Kansas City, Missouri. Actually, their variation on it uses a device called the "Toddy" but the cold brewing principles explained earlier in the book still applies if you are up for the challenge of making it yourself.

Hops are pretty strong, so using them in the coffee brewing process requires a delicate touch. They also work better with a coffee that has less body/acidity and more fruity flavors to make sure the coffee and the hops compliment each other. It is an interesting drink that will definitely remind you of beer, especially if you are fond of IPAs.

Aged coffee doesn't just means digging the beans your aunt brought back from Costa Rica two years ago out of the back of a kitchen cabinet. Properly aged coffee needs to be in a carefully controlled environment. Aging needs to be done before roasting as well. Once the beans are roasted, they immediately start to release the internal oils and gasses that you would prefer go into your cup, so it doesn't make much sense to try and age roasted coffee beans in an effort to improve enjoyment of your coffee.

Although I am skeptical of trendy coffee variations as a general rule, I do enjoy trying them when I get a chance. Even when the new drink does not impress me, I rarely regret trying new things and expanding my own horizons. More often than not, there is a chance to learn more about the world of coffee through the experience by asking questions about the drink itself or by analyzing my own impression of the drink and trying to identify what I did and did not like about it. I also like to think about questions like: Is there anything interesting about this that could be useful for the coffee I make at home? Okay, so, I did not like it, but who *would* like it?

This process ultimately increases the enjoyment and satisfaction I get out of coffee.

CHAPTER FIVE

Coffee Recipes

How NOT to make Green Coffee Extract

From the "Decisions I immediately regretted" Department

Okay, I admit, it's not a good idea to go off trying every new health fad that comes along, especially when it comes to those promising to help melt belly fat. Still, I was intrigued by recent medical studies touting the benefits of green coffee extract.

Researchers still cant say for sure why green coffee extract seems to help people lose weight, but the working theory is this: chlorogenic acid, one of the thousand or so various chemicals in coffee, has properties that blocks glucose absorption, which then aids weight loss.[38] Regardless, I happened to hear this news after receiving a fresh batch of green coffee beans so I set my mind to experimenting.

The first challenge was figuring out how the extract is made. Not surprisingly, doing an Internet search for "green coffee extract" turned up lots of ads for sketchy supplement websites and not a lot of advice for actually making it.

I scoured the web periodically for a couple weeks trying to find recipes. I found a couple sites that suggested just taking a handful of the green beans and boiling them, but there's no way that boiling unground green beans for a few minutes would extract much from them.

I even asked my brother, a physician and chemistry freak, about good ways to make an extract and he suggested grinding with a mortar and pestle and then, you guessed it, boiling. Unfortunately the mortar and pestle my wife uses for grinding spices was far to small and dainty to even make a dent in the rock hard green coffee shells.

Finally, I happened upon a blog post on Tim Ferriss' blog that laid out a reasonable method of extraction:

"Simply grind the green beans and prepare in a

French press like normal coffee. Alternatively, place the ground beans in water in the sun to brew iced coffee."[39]

Grind and prepare like normal coffee, eh? I had only very briefly considered using my grinder, dismissing the possibility early on assuming that it probably wouldn't be wise to put the rock hard little seeds through my grinder. But since this guy on the Internet says it's okay, then it should be fine, right? Well, it was a starting point. I got about 20 grams of coffee beans, dumped them in my grinder, set the dial... and immediately regretted it. The sounds coming out of my prized burr grinder made my stomach churn. It didn't sound like it broke, more like it was breaking. I shut off the grinder about halfway through the batch of beans.

Aside from nearly destroying my grinder, it did a really bad job of grinding. I suspect that a cheap blade grinder may actually be better suited for this job than a burr grinder. If nothing else, it would have been less of an investment in this half-baked idea. Regardless, I took the grounds and dumped them in an apparatus my wife has on hand for making tea:

As you can see there are some roasted coffee grounds in the mix too that were apparently leftover from my last batch of coffee. I just decided to leave it be rather than clean it all up and start over again. I figured the worst that could happen would be that my "extract" has a slight actual coffee flavor to it.

With that ready to go, I filled up the kettle and got things underway:

What I was making was something completely different from what I expected. The whole process was a lot more like making tea than an experimental chemical extract, but regardless, I was reasonably confident I was on the right track.

I boiled this mixture for a good long time, intent on extracting as much of the chlorogenic acid as possible, regardless of what it might taste like in the end. In hindsight, this might not have been wise. If chlorogenic acid gets destroyed in the roasting process, who is to say that it's not destroyed during boiling? While boiling temperature is far below the temperatures incurred during roasting (in excess of 500 degrees), I can't be sure.

When it had boiled for a really long time, I let it all cool and strained the liquid (it turned out that my wife's metal tea filter did little to hold in my green coffee grounds). I sampled a small amount of it and put the rest in the refrigerator to use in my morning smoothies. Did it taste good? Not at all. But it wasn't repulsive either. It's something easily tolerable by most people I suppose.

Would I advise other people to try this? Never. In retrospect, I wasted a lot of time, coffee beans, and probably took a couple years off of my grinder's life expectancy. As you have probably guessed by now, I have not ventured to try my hand at making green coffee extract again. If it does indeed turn out to be a beneficial supplement, I will most likely opt to just buy it from a reputable manufacturer and I recommend anyone thinking of trying it do the same.

Butter/Paleo/IF Coffee: Too True to be Good

Disclaimer: Nothing in this article should be taken as medical advice. The purpose is to share my own experiences with "Butter Coffee," and to shed some light on the confusing terms that easily get mixed up in discussions over the weight loss protocol. If you are interested in trying it, you should research the claims and research behind them for yourself and discuss any health concerns with a health professional before proceeding.

I've struggled with obesity pretty much my whole

life. Without getting into the whole story, a few years back I was finally able to lose weight and keep it off, but the weight has slowly been creeping back, especially over the past year. I've tried several things to reverse this to no avail. So when I heard about a particular coffee recipe as a weight loss aid, it seemed too good to be true. Still, since it was related to coffee I thought I'd test it out to see how it went. After experimenting with butter coffee and researching its claims (specifically about the coffee itself), I believe there is a grain of truth to it, but it is necessary to further define the relevant terms.

The Concept

The basic idea behind butter coffee is to minimize the negative side effects, while capitalizing on the benefits, of the intermittent fasting (IF) weight loss protocol. IF proponents, which fall roughly in the 'paleo' camp, claim that by restricting your daily caloric intake to a six hour window your body, for a bunch of sciencey reasons I don't fully understand (hey, I told you I'm not a doctor), helps you lose body fat. The butter coffee recipe claims to, by starting the morning with a big shot of healthy fats, kick your body into a ketosis state, causing it to burn fat, including stored fat, for fuel. At least that's my understanding of it.

The ingredients:

16 ounces (two cups) of black coffee made from

mold-free (more on this in a bit) coffee beans.

Up to 80 grams of *unsalted* grass fed butter or Ghee.

A spoonful of MCT or coconut oil (for more of an energy boost).

The method:

Pour all ingredients in a blender and blend it.

Drink

As you can see, it's not particularly complicated. In fact, a portable milk frother/blender will work just fine, though I haven't tried it myself. It is recommended to start with a smaller amount of both butter and oil, and gradually increase the dose.

The Claims about Moldy Beans

Before I get into my experience with butter coffee, I want to share my research regarding the beans. The claim is that 90% of the world's coffee beans have been exposed to mold, and that the mold leaves behind mycotoxins that are not burned away during roasting and are bad for us for a crapload of reasons. I've been suspicious about these claims about moldy coffee beans because A) it is discussed like it's some big cover-up going on in the coffee industry, B) sources about mold in coffee are not easily tracked down, and C) In all my reading about coffee, the word mycotoxin hasn't come up even once. In fact, I haven't been able to find a source for the claim that 90% of green coffee beans are exposed to mold, but, assuming it's true and that it's probably more of a problem in low quality beans destined to be made into instant coffee or pre-ground grocery store coffee cans, I also knew that instant coffee and robusta alone make up a huge percentage of the world's coffee. It seems to me that just avoiding low quality coffee, which isn't really that hard, would be enough to reasonably ensure that you're drinking that 10% of non-moldy beans.

The fact is, the coffee industry, or, more narrowly, the specialty coffee industry, worries a lot about mold in beans. It was very difficult to find academic sources on mold in coffee specifically, but I showed the claims to a World Barista Championship judge and a professional roaster that, together, made these points:

Mold is a problem because it substantially impairs the taste of coffee.

Sumatra coffee in particular is susceptible to mold because of it's unique processing (wet hulling). Nearly all Sumatra coffee has mold issues.

Mold is already highly undesirable in coffee beans, but even so they were skeptical of the claims of any health risks due to the high temperatures involved in roasting.

In other words, mold being a problem is no secret, although not for the reasons claimed. Even if the concern over mycotoxins are warranted, however, it's not as difficult as it is implied to avoid coffee that has been exposed to mold.

It is claimed that beans grown at higher elevation are safer from mold. The aforementioned coffee experts agreed that coffee grown at higher elevation is better, adding that it is for a whole host of reasons, only one of which is their being relatively free from mold.

The recipe's evangelists go a step further than this, though, by saying that you need to go beyond single origin (beans from a single country or region). It is argued that single estate is the best. In other words, beans from a single farm that have not been mixed with other beans to produce a bag of, for example "Kenya AA" coffee. Again, this is something that the specialty coffee industry is already doing. "Direct Trade" coffee is a practice that more and more specialty coffee companies are participating in, which is increasing the availability of single estate coffee all over the world. If you have a cafe in your town that has it's own roaster and offers drip coffee made at least two different ways, it's a good bet that they will have single estate roasted beans on hand. It's no accident that the people evangelizing for this method of drinking coffee also happen to sell their own brand of coffee beans, which are 'mold-free' of course, at a truly premium price.

I can summarize the recommendations about coffee beans in one word: DUH!!! Although myself and selected coffee experts technically agree with the recommendations, the reasons are completely different from what is suggested.

My recommendation: Just buy awesome coffee, roasted by highly reputable professionals. I can recommend Blue Bottle, Intelligentsia, 38th Parallel, or Stumptown (I haven't personally tried Stumptown but it's viewed as a kind of rebellious up-and-comer). These companies are relatively small operations that are in it for the love of coffee and bend over backwards to make sure the beans they sell live up to their reputation. In other words, they are among the top roasters on the planet, and the price is probably about the same.

If you really want to be cautious about the mold, you can follow the advice and specifically buy single estate Central American beans. If you can't find single estate beans, then single origin is probably good enough. Steer clear of Sumatra entirely and try to avoid African and Asian beans. I personally think this is overkill, but it's not going to hurt you, and there's no reason to spend big money on proprietary brand coffee unless, for you, the high price is worth the convenience of not having to shop around.

My Story

The first couple of days using the butter coffee (again, just to clarify, I'm talking about the recipe, not the proprietary beans. I just used the Kenya AA I had on hand -I roast my own coffee-, which advocates would probably strongly disapprove of due to low elevation and the processing method), I can say there was a very noticeable effect on my energy level.

I was full of energy and very focused, without any jitteriness. I don't usually notice much difference in how I feel from food, vitamins, or even doctor-prescribed pain killers, but I felt the effects of the coffee before I even finished the first cup. I'm not a morning person at all and generally take a while to get going, but my first cup of butter coffee had me up and at 'em.

Unfortunately by the fourth day this effect was barely noticeable. I still had enough energy to get through until my first meal, just not the boost that I enjoyed initially. Also, it continued to work pretty much as advertised in terms of appetite suppression. I didn't really get hungry until later in the afternoon. I didn't follow the IF/paleo diet protocol exactly, I just tried to eat as clean as I could and cut down on, but not eliminate, carbs.

I started at 112 kgs. On the morning of the fifth day on butter coffee I weighed myself and I was 108.7kgs. I couldn't believe it, but I already noticed my pants and dress shirts were fitting way better. A few days later, I weighed myself again and was 108.3 kgs, but the night before weighing myself I'd gorged a bit on account of a family gathering with the in-laws. Most meals I eat are some kind of meat (not grass fed or anything special) and lots of veggies. I live in Korea, so it's all Korean food, and I just limit myself to a few spoons' worth of rice.

I also train in Brazilian Jiu Jitsu three mornings a week. In terms of energy for the workout, I've probably had MORE energy than usual. I read that if you work out in the morning, you should just have a protein shake after the workout, and then your regular 2pm meal so that's what I've been doing.

Using butter coffee in the morning combined with intermittent fasting, I was able to cut about ten pounds in a couple weeks before departing for the U.S. to visit family for the holidays (and subsequently gain all the weight back binging on Christmas cookies and Kansas City barbecue). This was all in the span of just a few weeks.

I'm back on the protocol now and, for me, the weight loss seems to have slowed, but is still very effective. I can't attest to the claims about gaining muscle mass on the protocol because I haven't have a body fat analysis check, but I'm excited by the results that I've seen, even if it does slow down to a more normal pace from now on. I plan to continue drinking butter coffee in the mornings for the foreseeable future.

What about the taste? Well, if you are already a specialty coffee convert and usually drink it black, you're not going to be enthralled with the taste. That being said, it's not horrible unless you use the wrong kind of butter. I accidentally used salted grass fed butter exactly once and the taste was so bad that I gagged. For that matter, it's no use stressing out about the exact method for brewing the coffee either, as the butter entirely overpowers any subtle flavors and scents to the coffee. I use my Clever to brew, but I don't stress out about the timing. In fact, since I'm not concerned about preserving the flavors of the coffee, rather than make two separate batches of coffee, I've been experimenting with longer steep times (3-4 minutes). If you're going to try butter coffee for weight loss, you're just going to have to accept that you'll be ruining perfectly good coffee for it, but you can always enjoy a cup of the real deal later in the day.

Summary

I will continue to personally drink, and endorse, Butter Coffee, but with qualifications.

There are two parts to the coffee that should be considered separately: There's the beans themselves (proprietary, brand name beans), and then also the butter coffee recipe using grass-fed butter and MCT oil. I believe claims are vastly overstated in regards to the danger of mold in beans. On the other hand, I personally experienced very rapid weight loss by blending a relatively large amount of grass fed unsalted butter and a spoonful of coconut oil in my regular ol' morning coffee and not eating again until 2pm (Intermittent Fasting). As for the taste of the concoction, well, let's just say it's nothing to write home about, although not as bad as it sounds.

"Umpkinpay Icespay" Latte

Although I've never been one to try those recipes you see floating around social media that copycats your favorite ice cream sandwich or store brand cookie, I couldn't help but get curious when my sister-in-law, Jenni Ward, shared a recipe for a coffee drink recipe that people in North America clamor for every Fall.

Indeed, as much as I rail against adding sugary, milky, concoctions to your coffee, even I, under the influence of yearly homesickness, succumbed to temptation and gave this a whirl.

The recipe, from her blog (GingeredWhisk.com), is as follows:

Ingredients
1 1/2 cups water
1 1/2 cups sugar
4 cinnamon sticks
1 tsp ground nutmeg
1/2 tsp ground cloves
3 tbsp pumpkin puree

Combine the water and sugar in a medium saucepan and heat over medium-high heat, stirring occasionally, until the sugar has completely dissolved.

Toss in the cinnamon sticks and whisk in the rest of the spices and the pumpkin puree.

Cook for about 5 minutes, stirring frequently, without letting the mixture come to a boil.

Remove from heat and allow to sit for 10-15 minutes.

Strain the syrup through a fine mesh strainer or cheesecloth into a container of your choice.

Store in the refrigerator.

I had to make a few tweaks to the recipe, living in Korea as I do. First, the typical "sweet pumpkin" that is easily found in North America is not so easy to find here in Asia. I substituted a smaller, greener, version and it worked just fine.

Second, cinnamon sticks are, apparently, illegal to order from abroad so I had to go with ground cinnamon. After several batches I figured out that a single teaspoon of ground cinnamon is enough to do the job, but I suspect that could even be dropped to a half teaspoon.

Third, don't you ever let that mix boil. On my first attempt I didn't pay close enough attention and the resulting syrup was very gooey and didn't mix well in a cup of coffee. To eliminate all boiling risk I just got in the habit of never letting the temperature setting rise above "low."

Finally, make sure to use quality ingredients. My first batch of the syrup was so bad I almost gave up. Luckily I decided to give it a second shot when fresh spices I had ordered arrived a few days later.

I've tried the syrup many different ways, and I think filling the cup halfway up with milk, half with coffee, two tablespoons of the syrup, and then some whipped cream on top turned out pretty good, and it seems to work both hot and on ice.

My favorite way to enjoy this syrup, however, wasn't with coffee at all; it was mixed in with maple syrup for pancakes.

TAKING IT UP ANOTHER NOTCH

If you've made it this far and you're hungry for more, this final chapter is going to point you in the right direction.

I'm not going to recommend that you go out and blow your paycheck on all the various methods of coffee brewing. Rather, I'd recommend focusing all of your energy on just one, with the goal of becoming an expert on that particular method, then starting with another one. Regardless of which method you've chosen to commit to, to really take things to the next level, I'd highly recommend the following purchases:

    1)   A high quality burr grinder. This is not really optional. If you're not making espresso, I can recommend the Capresso Infinity, which I have used personally for several years. You could go with a manual burr grinder as long as you don't think you'll get tired of it. The nice thing is the manual grinders are portable (I love my

Hario MSS1B and take it and my Aeropress with me whenever I travel overnight).

2) Next is to start carefully monitoring your water temperature. This means keeping a dedicated thermometer on hand. This is so important that I include it in my portable coffee setup that I described above. Most methods of brewing coffee require water somewhere between 190-205 degrees Fahrenheit.

3) A digital scale. If you are to the point where you can taste the differences in various single origin coffees and roasts, you need to start paying careful attention to doseage and extraction.

With the necessary equipment in place, it's time to start studying coffee in greater detail. I recommend following these steps:

1) Experimentation. Start tweaking and experimenting with your brewing method. While I recommended some basic methods in the second part of this book, there's more than one way to skin a cat and what you're trying to do is learn as much about your own taste preferences as you are about the coffee itself. Go on your favorite search engine and check out various methods. Favor methods suggested by blogging baristas, roasters, etc, rather than generic recipe/cooking sites.

2) Read up on coffee theory. SweetMarias.com is a particularly good site for learning about various single origin coffees and the roasts at which they shine. CoffeeGeek.com, on the other hand, is strongest in its forums and discussions about high end equipment (so if you're thinking of investing a couple grand in a high end espresso maker, I'd go here first). Finally, blogs

such as PerfectDailyGrind.com consistently put out quality educational content guaranteed to teach you something new every day.

3) There are several books that I can recommend about coffee's history and geopolitics. You can see them all in the special section of my website I made for you (www.CoffeeistManifesto.com/readers), but the two books *Uncommon Grounds* and *The Devil's Cup* are great places to start. Both books are packed with information about the history of coffee and its influence on our culture. I have a preference for *Uncommon Grounds*, but it is also a much heftier, almost academic, read, while *The Devil's Cup* is more of a travelogue.

4) When it comes to the science of brewing coffee, legendary barista and coffee shop owner Scott Rao has written two books that can together be considered the Bibles of making coffee. The two books are called *The Professional Barista's Handbook* and *Everything but Espresso*. At first glance, the books are a tad pricey and not really very long. Although you could conceivably read through them in one afternoon, in order to actually retain the goldmine of coffee science contained in these books, you'll need to go back and reference them over and over again. Think of them more like a training manual designed for working baristas.

5) Look for chances to take cupping classes. These classes, roughly equivalent to a wine tasting class, will really open your eyes to the world of coffee and help you to point out the subtle differences in coffees.

6) What better way to learn than by jumping in head first? Working part time in a local coffee shop will get you neck deep into coffee methods, business, and community.

Also, make sure to check out CoffeeistManifesto.com/readers which has direct links to all my recommended products.

ACKNOWLEDGEMENTS

Although she is merely weeks old, my daughter inspires me in a way that I couldn't have imagined. Ever since finding out that she was coming, I have been driven in a way that I never have been before. It is hard to put into words, but when I leave this earth, be it 60 years from now or tomorrow, I want to have something physical out there in the world for her to hold in her hands and, through that 'work,' feel in the presence of her father. A book, hopefully multiple books, seems like a great way for her to know and communicate with me when I can't be there in her moment of need.

It goes without saying that the completion of this book would not have been possible without the love and support of my wife, Hwasuk Kim. I owe her far more than I could ever repay, but I will keep trying every day as we grow old together.

As I am primarily self-taught in the world of coffee, an infinite amount of thanks is due to those that I learned from myself. I have already mentioned SweetMarias.com and Coffeegeek.com, but there are many other forums and websites I have scoured over after finding them on the Internet and then couldn't find again. One blog that I come back to time and time again is Frshgrnd.com, run by Aaron Frey. Mr. Frey and I both frequented the coffee shops of Seoul around the same period of time and, although we've never met face to face, we have had lots of informative interactions online.

At a time when I believed that my creativity and writing ability was dried up forever, Joe McPherson invited me to contribute to his blog, ZenKimchi.com, writing about something I loved: Coffee. The writing I did for ZenKimchi became the inspiration for this book and if it wasn't for Joe, I'm not sure the idea for this book would have come to mind.

I am enormously grateful to my cover designer, Jake Clark and feel very fortunate to have found an artist that intuitively understood what I was going for. If anyone that is reading this happens to be needing a logo, business card, book cover, etc, find this man and give him your money. Similarly, my friend Luis Rico-Costillo's help with the photography was indispensable. Information on his photography can be found at WaypointPhoto.com.

Update for 2015: The new edition of the book would not have happened without the support of my friend Shawn Roe, the brains behind the solar energy website www.sroeco.com/solar and his talent for motivation. Nor would I have been able to catch up with the changes in the world of self-publishing in as short a time frame as I did if it were not for Brendon Hufford (HustleHeart.co) introducing my to Dave Chesson and the amazing resources he provides at Kindlepreneur.com. Gentlemen, I am enormously grateful to you.

ABOUT THE AUTHOR

Steve is, and always will be, a midwestern American man at heart. He prides himself in his Kansas City roots and keeps close ties there no matter how far, or for how long, he roams.

He is also a writer and a lifelong lover of learning. In his decade in South Korea, Steve has blogged on the topic of coffee at Korean food blog ZenKimchi.com, learned Korean, co-founded a start up import business profiled in the book *The New Korea*, created a popular informational website for expats in Korea and guest lectured on the topics of job interviews, the OPIc English exam, and academic publishing at Universities and corporations across Korea.

Currently Steve is teaching in the Political Science and International Relations Department at Chosun University in Gwangju, South Korea. He is reachable via Steve@CoffeeistManifesto.com

ENDNOTES

[1] Allen, Stewart Lee (1999). *Devil's Cup.*

[2] Allen, Stewart Lee (1999). *Devil's Cup.*

[3] http://loxcel.com/sbux-faq.html

[4] http://consumerist.com/2007/02/consumer-reports-mcdonalds-coffee-better-than-starbucks.html

[5] http://view.koreaherald.com/kh/view.php?ud=20120717001049&cpv=0

[6] http://en.wikipedia.org/wiki/Starbucks#Market_strategy

[7] http://seattletimes.nwsource.com/html/

businesstechnology/2003505497_union02.html

[8] http://web.archive.org/web/20080324210344/ http://ca.news.yahoo.com/s/capress/ starbucks_tipping_suit

[9] Schultz, H., & Yang, D. J. (1997). *Pour your heart into it, how Starbucks built a company one cup at a time.*

[10] Main Street Cafe has since opened up in my hometown of Independence, and I enjoy it when I'm in the neighborhood. Also, The Roasterie, in nearby Kansas City has made it to the top of various 'America's best coffee shops'-type lists and I enjoy it greatly as well. But both of those are substantially farther away than the Starbucks up the street.

[11] Bates, Robert H., et. al. *Analytical Narratives.* Princeton University Press. 1998. p. 197

[12] http://www.ico.org/history.asp

[13] http://www.ico.org/show_faq.asp?show=8

[14] Bohman, Mary. "The International Coffee Agreement: a tax on coffee producers and consumers?" 1999.

[15] Cardenas, M., 1994, Stabilization and redistribution of coffee revenues: A political economy model

of commodity marketing boards, Journal of Development Economics 44, 351-380.

[16] Cycon, Dean. *Javatrekker: Dispatches From the World of Fair Trade Coffee.* Oct. 17, 2007. Chelsea Green Publishing. Kindle Edition.

[17] United States Department of Agriculture, Code

of Federal Regulations: Title 7, Vol. 3, Chapter 1, Parts 205.202 through 205.206.

[18] Mutersbaugh T, 2002, "The Number is the Beast: a Political Economy of Organic-Coffee Certification and Producer Unionism" *Environment and Planning A* **34**(7) 1165 – 1184

[19] Soto-Pinto Lorena, Romero-Alvarado Yolanda, Caballero-Nieto Javier, Segura Warnholtz Gerardo. Woody plant diversity and structure of shade-grown-coffee plantations in Northern Chiapas, Mexico. Rev. biol. trop [revista en la Internet]. 2001 Dic [citado 2012 Ago 11] ; 49(3-4): 977-987. Disponible en: http://www.scielo.sa.cr/scielo.php?script=sci_arttext&pid=S0034-77442001000300018&lng=es.

[20] Organic Trade Association. August 2009. "Facts About Organic Coffee." http://www.ota.com/organic/organic_and_you/coffee_collaboration/facts.html

[21] Transfair USA. 2008. http://www.transfairusa.org/pdfs/almanac_2008.pdf . Page 9.

[22] Organic Trade Association. August 2009. "Facts About Organic Coffee." http://www.ota.com/organic/organic_and_you/coffee_collaboration/facts.html

[23] **Social Dimensions of Organic Coffee Production in Mexico: Lessons for Eco-Labeling Initiatives**

David Barton Bray, Jose Luís Plaza Sánchez, Ellen Contreras Murphy

Society & Natural Resources

Vol. 15, Iss. 5, 2002

[24] Rice, Robert A. "Noble goals and challenging terrain: organic and fair trade coffee movements in the global marketplace." Journal of Agricultural and Environmental Ethics. 2001-03-01. pp. 39-66. Springer Netherlands.

[25] Cycon, Dean. *Javatrekker: Dispatches From the World of Fair Trade Coffee*. Oct. 17, 2007. Chelsea Green Publishing.Kindle Edition.

[26] http://www.hasblog.co.uk/direct-trade-sucks

[27] Cycon, Dean. *Javatrekker: Dispatches From the World of Fair Trade Coffee*. Oct. 17, 2007. Chelsea Green Publishing. Kindle Edition.

[28] Organic Trade Association. August 2009. "Facts About Organic Coffee." http://www.ota.com/organic/organic_and_you/coffee_collaboration/facts.html

[29] Cycon, Dean. *Javatrekker: Dispatches From the World of Fair Trade Coffee*. Oct. 17, 2007. Chelsea Green Publishing.

[30] Photo by Luis Rico-Costillo

[31] http://www.ico.org/making_coffee.asp

[32] http://coffeegeek.com/guides/howtouseapourover

[33] Photo Credit: Luis Rico-Costillo

[34] Photo Credit: Luis Rico-Costillo

[35] Photo Credit: Luis Rico-Costillo

[36] http://www.columbiamissourian.com/stories/2010/01/11/coffee/

[37] http://stores.lakotacoffee.com/StoreFront.bok

[38] http://www.webmd.com/diet/news/20120328/

green-coffee-beans-may-aid-weight-loss

[39] http://www.fourhourworkweek.com/blog/
2012/05/23/10-uncommon-superfoods-from-the-world-of-
ultra-endurance/#more-6835

Made in the USA
Lexington, KY
13 August 2016